I'll Pray for You

and Other Outrageous Things

Said to Disabled People

Hannah Setzer

I'll Pray for You and Other Outrageous Things Said to Disabled
People
By Hannah Setzer

Cover by Katrina Taggart-Hecksher

Printed in USA

First Edition

For Meatball & Baby Hannah

Table of Contents

PART IV The Moon is Round and Other Moments of Advocacy and Motivation

Preface

I was in Mexico, sitting beside my private pool. You may close this book now and think, *Dang, she's a spoiled brat. I'm over this.* I promise you this isn't my normal state, but here I sit. Halfway through our vacation, I had a little existential crisis. If you've read the back cover of this book, you'll know I'm a person who does a lot of things. I prefer the term festive human: advocate, dreamer, wife, mother, queen of a small business, executive director of a nonprofit, farmer, and writer. Add to the list aspiring locksmith, mini cow owner, TED Talk giver, and potential moon-goer. Anyway, I was having an existential crisis because I someone recently told me that I do too much and need to focus my energy on one thing. That's kind of hard to do when I have all these humans and animals to take care of and medical bills to pay and fun to be had, so I didn't appreciate the advice too much. Also, I tried having one focus in 2021. My first focus was to get a book deal. I got thirty rejections and cried a lot and didn't talk about how hurt I was because of it. Then, my husband and I started a nonprofit to build an accessible playground in our country town. That became my only focus. I poured over online commercial land listings, called dozens of realtors and lenders, and mostly just got laughed at by banks. I felt like Lorelai Gilmore when she tried to open the Dragonfly Inn and said that she could still hear the banks laughing hours after her meetings with them to obtain a loan. I started crying every day and feeling very rejected. Everyone praised me for having such a great idea and noble cause, but no one could help us. Hopefully, by the time this book is released, we'll have bought land and built an accessible playground and garden. If 2021 taught me anything, it is that having *one* focus in life is not for me. It leads to a lot of crying because I want things to happen instantly, and maybe deep down, I think that I'm a relatively good person and think things *should* happen how I want and when I want. Back to my existential crisis... I acted like nothing was wrong (lies, all lies) and told Brandon how I felt like a failure. I couldn't get a book deal. I couldn't make million-dollar dreams come true in seven months. I was seeking hits of dopamine from new projects left and right because I couldn't bear to face more Zillow listings or more literary agent rejection letters. Brandon said to focus on one thing. I told him that was not an option. He said to flip a coin and focus on whatever landed, and then brandished a penny. I told him I didn't want to do that either. Then, he got mad at me for rejecting all his ideas, which was probably an acceptable response after he let me cry on his shoulder. Then, in a huff, he said, "Why can't you start writing again?" and I said, "Because I'm scared!" (which, hello, I had not even admitted to myself), so I was shocked—and a little mad—that my husband was able to get me to admit this. He asked what I feared, and I said more rejection. He very plainly said, "I don't know who told you that you deserved a book deal or that it would be easy to get, but they were wrong." Then, I punched him in the nose and walked out. Just kidding. I just stared agog at him. He said, "Hannah, why do you want to write a book?" and I told him because I know I have a story to tell inside me, and it's been bursting to come out for . . . oh, like eighteen years at least, starting with my Xanga and LiveJournal blogs. He sat up and looked at me and said, "Then write. Why are you letting thirty literary agents out of the millions of literary agents in the world tell you that you can't write a book? Write the dang book and self-publish it. You can't be mad at them for saying 'No!'" Then, I admitted (again, a surprise to me) that I was mad at *myself* for not doing the dang thing I felt called to do and instead shrinking back in fear and shielding myself from more rejection by ceasing to write at all. As someone who has been stubborn from the time she was knitted together in her mama's womb, and who has rejected a lot of people who rejected her—Hi, the entire medical community who told my mom and dad I wouldn't live—I was somehow brought down by lit agents over email.

Then I opened up my Instagram DMs and a dude sent me a message saying:

> "Hey, I saw on one of your posts you were looking for a book deal. I'm a ghost writer and would love to help you make your dreams come true. Can we chat?"

…and I looked around and thought this had to be a cosmic joke. Before my talk with Brandon, I had asked God, "Hey, I need just a little sign to tell me if I should start writing again?"

. . . and then the talk with Brandon happened and then this DM. I also texted my friend, Ashley, and said "OMG is this a sign?!" She said "maybe."

Then, I got a text from my mom about a note I had written her a few days before, and she said, "You're a good writer."

Hello, is that a sign too? I reckon they had to be. *Then*, Brandon was all "Hey, come look at the moon. I think it's a full moon," which, if you know me, you know I love gazing at the moon. Don't worry; I'll tell you *why* later.

I was like, "Okay, God, hello, I see you."

Now, here I am. Day one (of like hundreds of days) of working on this book thing again. I reread my proposal I sent to agents a year ago, and I love it. I love the girl that wrote it. I'm proud of the girl that wrote it. But she's no longer me. She's faced rejection on bigger levels than a boyfriend she had in her 20s. She's dreamed bigger dreams. She's started new businesses, found her creative side thanks to her Cricut, yelled at social workers until her son's adoptions were all finalized, and milked goats daily for a year.

It's hard and humbling and scary to take your dreams into your own hands. Relying on others to accept or reject me was nice because *I did the thing.* I submitted the proposal. I called the realtor. I made offers on land. My fate was in someone else's hands. When you take dreams into your own hands, it means a lot of freedom but also a lot of trusting yourself. I realized, in the twenty-four hours since I cried on Brandon's shoulder in a hotel bed, that I didn't trust myself. I didn't trust myself to do the work if someone wasn't making me. I didn't trust myself to accomplish this big thing that I'd talked about for years. I didn't have a deadline. I didn't have a cash advance. I didn't have people praising my work. It was just me—in a hammock in Mexico (for three more days)—chasing my dreams. Sure, Brandon was there interrupting me every five minutes to tell me about his Stephen King book, but it's just me sharing my story with you. You people that hopefully will read these words. The thousands of people over the last eighteen years that have said, "Oh, you should write a book!" I did remind Brandon of all of you when he asked me who told me I should write a book, but since I couldn't name very many of you (sorry), he said that was nice, but I shouldn't feel entitled due to you. I should feel entitled due to *me*. My dreams. My desires. My story to tell. It's been bursting inside of me for years. Every day I think about writing (as if that has never been a sign LOL), but I've been scared. Scared of big dreams. Scared to be vulnerable in more than 2,200 characters on an Instagram caption.

If you've got big dreams, I get you. I see you. It's freaking hard. Harder than I ever thought. When crying to Brandon, I legitimately wailed, "I'm overwhelmed having so many big dreams. It's too much to handle." Ya feel me? It's okay if you don't. All dreams are valid and good, and chasing them, big or small, is hard as crap. This is your permission slip. No expiration dates. Permission to dream really big dreams. I'm here to extend hope to you that you can live the rebellious life you want and dream the big dreams you want. You're gonna get told no. I am still going to get told no. But today, we say, who cares? We are living our best, truest, most rebellious life (like, don't commit crimes . . . but like do the things that make you feel alive . . . if committing crimes makes you feel alive . . . get a cat or something, just don't do that). We need your dreams. We need the rebellion. We need the hope that we can be who we want to be. We need the ability to chase our size XXXS - XXXL dreams.

Introduction
I'll Pray for You and Other Outrageous Things Said to Disabled People

If I had a dollar for every time someone told me, "I'll pray for you," I'd be rich. Literally a millionaire. Daily, I receive messages from very kind and well-meaning people telling me they are praying for me. People that I don't know but who have just seen me on social media. *Seen* is the keyword here. They see my face and equate how I look with needing healing. These messages are typically unsolicited, and I don't really think anyone should need an explanation as to why you shouldn't message people and tell them you're praying for them when they haven't indicated they need prayer, but maybe some people do! Every time I bring this topic up, though, I get a *lot* of feedback and strong opinions from people, so maybe we do need an explanation. Let me say straight up, I believe in

God and Jesus, I believe in prayer, I believe in meditation, and I believe in healing. All those things are explicitly true in my own life, but I still don't think you need to tell people (unsolicited) that you are praying for them without any prompting. If you want to pray, do it. Your prayers don't count any more or less if you tell the person.

There is a difference here, friends. I am certain that every single day of my life, probably before I was born, people have prayed for me. My parents, my grandparents, and countless kind humans have prayed for me. I think that's incredible, and it brings me to tears to think about it. There have been innumerable times that I've gotten cards in the mail from people from my grandma and grandpa's church in Tennessee telling me I'm being prayed for. There is more than one prayer shawl that has been knitted for me by incredible women of faith as they prayed for me. Whether you, too, believe in God or not, having faith like that is impressive. I'm inextricably grateful for each of my days being covered in prayer. These are beautiful and welcomed, and I am so grateful for them. Knowing all that, please trust me in what I'm sharing.

Prayer itself is not the issue. Pray for me, pray for Beyoncé, pray for whatever you and your higher power want to pray for. One message I received still sticks out to me; it said, "I will pray for you. I think God should be with you and heal you. Because trying matters. And miracles do happen." Whew, did I lose my mind! I love Jesus and God, and I know they are with me. I don't think I'm not "healed" because I'm not trying hard. Trying for what? Trying for faith? Trying to be a good person? The Jesus I believe in, who hung with prostitutes and degenerates, never asked anyone to try harder before he interacted with them or healed them. Trying is the antithesis of the gospel of Jesus, so I'm not for that language at all. I'm a relatively good human being. I don't do any one specific thing in life because I'm trying to be healed or earn jewels on my crown in heaven. I was just raised by good people and try to be a good, inclusive, and affirming person! I really do believe the people who share messages about "praying for me" have good intentions. I don't think they do so out of malice, anger, or harm. The line, "I think God should be with you and heal you," makes me laugh and feel insane all at the same moment. I, too, think God should be with me. And let me check, yep, I think she's right here with me. Thanks, God.

This person saw my face, probably amidst mindless scrolling on social media, and assumed that because of how I looked, I needed to be healed. They didn't know my medical history, didn't know that I was born with this condition, didn't know that the tube in my neck and tube in my belly sustain me and give me the ability to hike mountains, travel internationally, parent these kids, and move my body every day. They just saw foreign objects in holes that surgeons cut in my body and assumed I needed healing to remove them. Similar to how mobility aids help people get around in the world, my feeding tube lets me live. And, I live a dang good life. There is nothing to actually heal me from. I guess healing the thousands upon thousands of cysts in my head and neck so I could swallow? And maybe healing from the insane scar tissue in my head that has bent multiple titanium plates and screws in more than one reconstructive surgery that also pulls my lower lip down so it doesn't touch the top one? I don't ever let myself think about these possibilities and changes because this imaginary person wouldn't be me. I can't picture what I'd look like if my lips touched and my mouth wasn't open. Some days it would be nice to have a belly that wasn't full of scars and a feeding tube, but after thirty-two years, I don't think I'd want to learn how to eat by mouth and figure out what I like or don't like and pay for food at restaurants. Brandon fell in love with me and how I look, not how I'd look if I were ever to be *healed.* He didn't go into this relationship, nor did any previous partners, with the hope or assumption that anything would ever be any different. Yes, my face is different, but honestly, if it wasn't how it is, I would be just another basic white girl. Eating without a feeding tube would maybe feel more inclusive, but I couldn't do things like blend up leftover chili, rice, some mango, eggs from our chicken, and whatever else I found in the fridge. I get to eat as healthy as I want (or don't want—here's to blending up pizza) and live my best life. Also, I can eat while I'm sleeping or in the shower, so really, who is losing out? All these things have made me who I am, and yes, my character can use some healing, but on a regular day-to-day basis, my body doesn't need healing.

Once I was in a church in Colorado, and as I was leaving when the service ended, a woman came up to me and blocked my path. She put her hands on my head (without asking) and started praying over me. She prayed for healing and recovery and then started speaking in tongues. I moved her hands off me *real* quick and was very firm in stating I didn't need to be healed. Could I be healed from my controlling behavior, quick tongue, and the short temper that rears its ugly head? Sure thing! But that woman didn't know any of those not-so-fun things about me. She just saw that I looked different and maybe heard that my voice sounded different. She assumed, without knowing me or having any interaction with me, that it was her job to cast out whatever demon was in me so my face would become *normal*? She was very taken aback as to why I wouldn't want her prayers and didn't understand why I dismissed her and scurried away so quickly. What if I had been someone exploring their faith and coming to church for the first time, and that's the experience I had? I imagine I would be so turned away from following Jesus after that. The number of assumptions this woman had based on my appearance and location is astounding.

I have talked to countless other disabled individuals who have the same story as me. It is not uncommon. Just because you don't have the audacity to invade someone's privacy like this (thank you!) doesn't mean others don't. It's absurd. I get the heebie-jeebies just thinking about this woman. This was years before we lived in a pandemic world, but hello, germs have always existed! I don't know where her hands had been. She didn't know where my head had been! What if I was very sweaty? If you and your higher power want to speak in tongues, that is your prerogative in life, but I want to know what is being said about me, to my face, behind my back, to a higher power, whatever, however. For all I know, she was cursing me! I don't play around with tongues. I don't care if she, or you, were praying to any specific higher power. I'm not here to debate religion or what is true or valid by any means, but I want to at least know what is happening whilst the prayers are going up.

Ableism is so deeply rooted in our society that people are conditioned to think that disabled equals bad or wrong or needing to be fixed. Without knowing a single fact, our minds snap to how a disability can be different, how it can be fixed, and what could make it better. Better tends to equal normal. I'm not sure I want to be better if that's the case. No disabled person needs to be. We weren't made to be clones. I want to be me, even if others think the *me* I am isn't something *they* would want to be. There are several stories in the Bible of disabled people interacting with Jesus and them being healed. I am here for miracles. Not the late-night televangelist miracles where you can pay your way, but real-life miracles. I am a miracle. No doctor thought I'd survive, and here I am, living the best life I know. I believe if Jesus wanted me to wake up tomorrow with lips that touched and could breathe and eat without tubes, he could do it. That'd be really cool. I don't pray for that, though. The thought has never crossed my mind. Don't get me wrong; I've spent time over the last thirty years asking why I was made this way but never asking for it to change. Perhaps instead of random messages, we need to let everyone lead the conversations that they are comfortable with having. I almost typed "we need to let disabled people lead," but honestly, we all need to let each other lead. We need to trust that every person is an expert in themselves and what they need and want from life. I love who I am. I love what I look like. My physical appearance does not need to be healed. Lots of other crap in my life does, but not my cute little face.

What you are about to read will come to you in chunks. Parts. Sections if you will. They are as follows:

Part I   Growing Up Stories and Medical Afflictions
Part II   Loving People and Animals
Part III Fitness: Intentional Movement Each Day
Part IV The Moon is Round and Other Moments of Advocacy and Agency

In each part you'll find chapters that I like to think of as essays. Each could stand on its own. In fact, I invite you to read each piece as its own essay. Go ahead, skip around, read one from each part. Start in the middle. Go crazy. Life is not linear and neither is reading this book. Of course, you can start at the beginning and read straight through. It's up to you. You get to choose. You are in

charge of your reading path and your dream seeking!
Let's do it!

Part I
Growing Up Stories and
Medical Afflictions

1

When the Rebellion Began

If you were to ask me when the rebellion in my life began it would be hard to give you an answer, as the rebellion in my heart began before my heart was even formed and beating. The rebellion began in a life before mine, with my mother. In January 1990 tiny embryo Hannah was formed, and I must say I`m very happy to know no details of the event. I'm not even sure how far along in my mom's pregnancy she found out that I was ~*special*~ but at some point, she did. She's not a very rebellious person by nature, she's actually like an angel on earth but she knew better than the doctors did for the first time that day. Mama always knows best. I can't imagine how scary it is to be pregnant, for the fourth time, with a baby that doctors were constantly telling her was not viable, was not worth it, and would not live. If it had been her first pregnancy, I'd think she was overly hopeful and brave, but because she had done these three times before and was still willing to take the risk, I'd say she's rebellious. So, you can say that being rebellious is really in my DNA. My dad was rebellious as a youth in plenty of ways so he certainly gets some credit too. They made the hard decision to stay the course with little embryo Hannah who turned into little fetus Hannah with a fat head and they persisted. Whether it be their belief that God had bigger plans, or their rebellious nature to go against the grain and to believe bigger and better things were to come (the bigger the setback the bigger the comeback and I don't think ANYONE can deny that my comeback has been anything less than great) but I'm grateful they were tenacious and installed that in me from before I entered this world. I was born in late September and was in the NICU for months. Having friends now that have babies in the NICU, I can't imagine how my parents did it with three other kids at home. I'm glad they did, though. My dad loves to tell the story about how on Halloween, he bought me a little skeleton costume, and my mom was not happy about it, so when she left the hospital, he and the nurses put it on me. See, I really was destined to be a rebel. Rebellious parents. Rebellious nurses. It's in my genes.

Growing up I had an incredible team of doctors. When I was born I can't even imagine the amount of panic and terror for the doctors that were working that day. I know that my condition, cystic hygroma, is rarely covered in medical classes or journals or books now, so I can't even imagine what it was like 32 years ago. But, I was born, and they figured things out minute by minute day by day and worked with my parents to ensure tiny Hannah kept on trucking. I wasn't in the clear immediately though just because I got my trach and feeding tube. The prognosis was still grim. Doctors were convinced that despite their best efforts, I wouldn't live to be one. Then I did. Then they said I wouldn't live to be five. I did. You can see a pattern here. They also said I wouldn't walk, talk, or be anything other than a bed ridden gal with a feeding tube. The doctors on my care team were some of the best in the entire country. I had plastic surgeons, otolaryngologists, infectious disease doctors, and more in constant communication with my mom and dad, but still there wasn't much hope. You surely know how this is going to go, I rebelled. I wasn't a fan of thinking that my life would be reduced to lying in hospital beds hooked up to tubes forever, not really having a life. Let me be explicitly clear, all lives have value and worth, and if that was what my life were to be like, I would have been equally worthy of living and taking up space, and my parents would have cared for me and done everything they needed to do forever. I am certain of those things. But, living a rebellious, joy and adventure filled life sounded better to me. So, the tenacity that was woven into my DNA took over, along with some stubbornness, and the privilege of incredible medical care (because let's be real, that's the real MVP here–not my desire to overcome) and I not only survived, but I thrived. I'll take credit for rebelling over most things, and people, in my life but all the credit for getting me to that point goes to the doctors and my parents who watched their baby girl undergo surgery after surgery, experimental drug trials, all kinds of therapies, and more doctors' appointments than most people have had in their lifetime before I turned one.

When I was in middle school (if you knew me in middle school, let's never speak of anything that happened in that time), I remember my mom sitting me down one afternoon and telling me, "Hannah, if you wanted to sit in your room the rest of your life and be mad about your life and how you look and sound, *no one* would ever question that in you." I don't recall what led up to that conversation, but I remember thinking it was preposterous even from the start. Why would I hide? Why would I be mad forever? Why would I want to be alone forever? I know my mama meant that I had every right to be mad. I had every right to be mad about the constant stares and being made fun of. It wasn't just normal middle school horrors; this was more, and she knew it. Her mama heart ran deep for her only daughter, wanted to protect me from everything in our ableist society, and wanted to give me an out. Never before had she said anything like this to me, so I'm guessing something really horrible happened that I've just blacked out. She was being the best mama there ever was and giving her baby girl with a deformed face an out, a *Pass Go and Collect $200 Card*, and was ready to stand by whatever decision I wanted to make.

If right then I had said, "Okay, I'm throwing in the towel, and this is it," I know she and my dad would have supported me. If I had chosen to sit on my bright yellow bedspread with orange and blue flowers in my neon green room and thrown myself the world's biggest pity party, they would have shut the door and backed away slowly. There was nothing else they could do. They knew they couldn't protect me from all the bullies, and they didn't want me to have to protect myself and explain myself day in and day out to people. Surely by then, they knew how exhausting it was for me to just exist in a society not built for anyone that deviated from the norm. They would have given answers to anyone who questioned why I had slowly disappeared into our home and away from life. They would have done whatever I needed them to do because they are really great parents. But, it was ingrained in my soul and my DNA to rebel. To not give in. To fight against what was expected of me again. My parents didn't *wish* that I would shy away from the world, but my disability could totally have made this acceptable and assumed to be true.

Nevertheless, she persisted. That day I didn't give up. I didn't give in. I didn't wave the white flag my parents extended to me. This is not the first time I rebelled and leaned into something hard. I've been rebelling since my inception in my mama's womb and every day after. I'm not sure how old I was when this conversation happened, but I still think about it often. Now that I don't live at my parent's house, I don't think the offer still stands, but I think the sentiment remains. If I needed to pack it all up and pack it in, close myself away in my house, leave social media and my friends behind, and curl up within myself due to the exhaustion and now the trolls on social media, I could. Brandon, my husband, wouldn't question it. He may not understand it, as he's only been around me for a few years now, and not as many as my parents had been at the time of that conversation, but he wouldn't question it. Society wouldn't question it. Society may actually prefer it.

My senior year of high school, I was on homecoming court. I would not say I was at all the most popular, coolest, smartest, or any "est" kid. I had friends in all different groups (Breaking news: I was in marching band and played the xylophone.), but I was overall kind and funny and clearly looked different than my 500+ other classmates in twelfth grade. I was voted onto the homecoming court and did all the cheesy things and then didn't get voted homecoming queen. Praise God. I never thought much of this, was just like, oh yeah, I had lots of friends, and some of my other friends were on the court too, and it was just a fun and funny thing. I told someone about it my freshman year of college, and they said, "Oh, you know you were just voted onto homecoming court because everyone felt sorry for you." This person didn't know me. Didn't go to my high school. Didn't know my peers. Didn't know who I had been twelve months prior in a little Virginia town. I felt like I had been punched in the gut. Never had I ever thought that was a true statement. That thought *literally* had never crossed my mind. I was stunned.

I want to tell you that I stood up for myself and denied that to be true, threw my cup of water into this girl's face, and never talked to her again. I want to tell you I was a rebel and said some un-Christian college words to her. I didn't. I stood there and let her say these horrible things over me. To her, it probably meant nothing. In the moment, it meant everything to me. Everything shifted. Was *she* just speaking to me because she felt sorry for me? Was everyone I had ever been friends with only friends with me because they felt sorry for me? Was I let into college because they felt sorry for me? Has my entire life been one big surprise pity party that everyone had invitations to but me?

Dang, I spiraled. It honestly took years, *years* to rebel against those thoughts. To reclaim those memories of high school as fun and funny ones, not ones clouded in pity, or embarrassment that everyone besides me was in on a joke. Thank goodness that changed, and now I can take hundreds of mean comments and DMs on Instagram a day, and they roll off my back like nothing. I do keep a list of the best ones in my notes app because some make me laugh from horror or shock. I read them aloud to my kids because I refuse to raise men who will treat anyone like that, in person or online. I was going to say I've grown thicker skin, but that's not true. I've grown softer. Able to see that this random college freshman was actually *way* more insecure about herself than I ever have been besides those few moments standing in front of her. I can see the hurt behind people's words on Instagram. I can see a glimpse into how they were raised. Fear of the unknown runs deep, y'all.

I've come a long way from that girl in her childhood bedroom and an even longer way from the little baby Hannah that was born in Northern Virginia. Yet, I must still rebel. Ableism is alive and well in society. I take up physical space in the world and digital space online. I show up daily on Instagram, where I'm met with trolls asking why I'm there, why my hideous face shows up on their pages, why does Instagram think I'm something (not someone, *something*) that anyone would want to see. I go to pick up my kids' medicines at CVS and stand in the pick-up line, and people physically react and recoil from me. I don't shrink back. We do not shrink back. I rebel and stand tall and firm and speak clearly and loudly. I have learned how to advocate for myself. I do not see my needs or asks or accommodations as something to be ashamed of. You know what, when I tell people what I need boldly, I'm never met with annoyance, disappointment, or shock. But, when I fall over myself apologizing, shrinking back, making my needs or wants smaller, sacrificing parts of myself for others to feel more comfortable, it always exacerbates the situation. Disabled people are not only allowed, but encouraged, to take up space. Society wasn't built for us—for people who look differently, talk differently, move differently.

Representation is tissue paper thin, and until that changes, I will always be stared at at the gas station. If our TV shows, movies, magazines, books, billboards, targeted social media ads, clothing websites, and cereal boxes ever centered disabled people, things would change. Typically, disabled people are only ever featured after they *have overcome* something. Make no mistake; my disability, specifically, is not something to overcome. Believe me; I've had at least sixty surgeries. That's why this isn't a typical overcoming story. Mine is a story of active rebellion and redemption. I've been redeeming my life from the words spoken over me before birth. You don't have to overcome something to live the life you want. You don't have to be *inspirational*; you don't have to run a marathon or overcome insane adversity. Be a freaking rebel right where you are. Stand up for the things you need to stand up for. Live your damn life, y'all.

Yesterday or even five minutes ago, someone may have said some insane thing to you online or in person. It took years for me to reclaim that conversation I had on a dorm floor fourteen years ago. I'm not saying it's always easy. But I am saying it's always worth it—to be true to yourself. To tell the world what you need. To take up the space you *deserve*. The rebellion and reclaiming are always worth it. You get the choice to rebel right here, right now. Rebel against your inner thoughts.

Let's reclaim some shit together.

2
The National Zoo/
I Can't Understand You

The first time I remember being made fun of was in kindergarten, specifically at the panda exhibit at the National Zoo. You may be surprised to hear that it wasn't actually the pandas making fun of me but a little boy who was about my age. He wasn't in our class; he was just with his parents, which was weird since it was a school day, and we were on a field trip, and he was clearly not. They were on the same guided tour as we were, which gave him ample time all day to get too close to me and to point and laugh at my face. I remember him asking his parents, not me, what was wrong with me and them shhh-ing him. At one point, he sidled up next to me and asked me directly, in a low whisper, "What's wrong with your face?" I had my lines rehearsed, as my parents had taught me since birth, to say, "Nothing is wrong with me; I was just born this way." Either he didn't understand me, or that answer didn't satiate his curiosity because he continued to ask. I didn't have any other language, though. That's all my parents ever taught me to say, that I was born this way. Now that I'm older, I can say a lot more, such as, "Go away," "Stop staring at me." But, as a little five-year-old, I didn't know I was allowed to be so assertive when people were making me feel uncomfortable.

Growing up, I always had a private nurse with me in school. She was around, essentially, to make sure I didn't die or that my feeding tube didn't explode. The burden was too much to ask of public school teachers, so private nurses were hired. Eventually, my nurse, Joan, caught on to this boy. While I wasn't bothered by it, she certainly was. At one point, she turned around and sternly told him to stop. She told him that I was fine and he needed to stop being so nosey. She was personally responsible for me physically and also emotionally that day. I remember her buying me a panda foldout fan from the gift shop to make me feel better, and I *LOVED* that fan. I opened and closed it and fanned myself for years until the cheap paper fell apart at the seams. I bet that fan is still somewhere at my parents' house to this day.

I don't remember feeling bothered by his persistence, but I do remember feeling exhausted by it. Having to continually explain over and over that I was normal, trying my best to get him to understand that I was okay, was exhausting. I was just trying to enjoy the animals kept in cages like everyone else. My parents always taught me it was rude to stare, so I didn't even think to stare back at him, which is a tactic I use with adults now. This was my first foray into being exhausted by having to prove myself to someone else. I am still having to prove myself every day—from gas station clerks to attorneys and judges in courtrooms. It is exhausting, as a human and in professional settings. Just yesterday, I dropped off my own product, from my own business, at a local grocery store that sells it, and I had to explain to *FOUR* different sales clerks who I was and why I was there with cases of the product. Maybe I didn't "look like" a business owner. When I'm in a courtroom in a suit advocating for a client or for my foster kids, I certainly "look like" a professional, but I still have to work at least twice as hard as my colleagues or my husband to be heard and taken seriously. Don't even get me started on trying to talk to the robots that big companies use on the telephone when you call a customer service number. Those robots exhaust me to tears usually. Yes, my speech is different, and yes, my face is different, but for the love, just assume if I'm in a room, I'm supposed to be there. Whether that room is a literal courtroom or the zoo. I belong in all spaces and deserve to be in all spaces. I also deserve not to have to explain myself or my existence to everyone else in those spaces.

Fast forward decades later, and I was chased down in a Tractor Supply parking lot by an employee trying to understand me. I had approached him asking for firewood, and the employee couldn't understand me, despite speaking slowly and enunciating my words to the best of my ability. I mimed chopping down a tree, I mimed warming my hands by a fire, I pointed to trees, and nothing worked. After several minutes of me speaking louder and slower each time, feeling like a fool, I walked away. Fuming, I walked back to my car. At some level, I was frustrated at him, unlike the boy at the zoo many years earlier. The boy at the zoo met me with only five years of frustration in my life, and the employee at Tractor Supply met me with thirty. He chased me down and begged me to help him understand. I finally wrote down 'wood' on my hand, and he understood. This seems like it would be a moment of elation that the two of us were finally on the same page, but I am jaded enough to know that probably wasn't the case.

The second he understood what I was asking him, he started speaking slowly to me and enunciating all his words, as if I couldn't understand him or as if I was less intelligent. Essentially, he equated my perceived lack of intelligence based on how I looked and how he interpreted my voice. He was very kind and tried his hardest to help me, but he didn't slow down and changed his demeanor until after the accommodation had been used. Only then did he seem to assume my ability or intelligence level. So, not only did I have to fight to be understood, but after I was understood, I had to fight to be taken as a serious customer. Just like the boy at the zoo, he wouldn't accept my initial answer that I was okay, despite being born this way. (Yes, I know, he wasn't asking why my face looked this way, but he was assuming my intelligence level and my perceived differences based on our brief interaction). All I wanted was some dang firewood to burn in my backyard with some pals.

You may think all this would make me insecure. It for sure makes me tired, but nothing about this makes me insecure. In the past thirty years, there has not been a day where I haven't been stared at or mocked. Life actually got a bit easier for me when COVID-19 occurred, and masks were mandated in Virginia. For the first time ever, I could hide my face on a day that wasn't Halloween, and everyone else was doing it too. Despite wearing a mask in public, I still have a capped tracheostomy tube sticking out my neck and sound slightly funny when I talk, but no one can see my lips stretched wide open over my teeth, unable to touch each other. I didn't get nearly as many stares as I went about my life. It was easy to think that maybe wearing a mask was the answer the whole time, but I know that isn't true. Hiding has never been the answer. Life is way too short to hide who we are.

Just as I have found my voice to speak up against people who ask too many questions or are mean, our country is developing its voice as well. There is more advocacy now than ever before, but it's also because there are more avenues to question, hurt, bully, and offend people than ever before. As a little girl, getting picked on at the zoo or the playground was all I had to worry about. These days kids can get picked on by millions of people all across the world at the tap of a finger. We speak out against all these horrors, but we give life to more and more pathways to have access to people. There is more representation now than ever, but it still comes at the cost of hurt people behind screens. A new kind of exhaustion sets in when you allow yourself to be public, and thousands of people are entering your home and saying whatever they want to via a four-inch iPhone screen.

The fight is worth it. I must rebel against all the haters and use my life and voice to stand up for myself—the five-year-old girl I never stood up for before and for all those little five-year-old kids with disabilities and medical conditions to come. I will not wave my white flag and let this society that wasn't built for us win. I will advocate on the playground and in the Tractor Supply parking lot with a man who is more than twice my age. The fight is worth it. The ability to extend hope to just one person that they can live the gloriously rebellious life they want—and deserve—is worth it. While my family is the bomb diggity, I don't think they'd take much credit for the life I lead now. My mama says all the time I'm way more fearless than she ever has been, which is not true, but I did carve this path for myself. And, I carve it every day. Dear reader, our paths are not the same, but I just need you to know that the wild and glorious life you desire is possible. We were not made to hide. We do not belong to those who shrink back. (Hebrews 10:39 New International Version).

3

A "Shocking" Adventure

When I was either a sophomore or junior in high school, I had an infection in the cysts in my face. These infections happened frequently, like once or twice a month. Usually, we could combat them with a trip down the road to my primary care doctor and some antibiotics, but sometimes they were really bad, and we had to call in the big guns . . . aka the infectious disease doctor. File this in the "Things most teenagers don't have" category: their own infectious disease doctor. It's interesting, though, because my medical condition is not a disease, but I guess because all my little cysts loved to rage off the insane amount of sugar and other processed crap in the eight cans of

PediaSure I consumed every day, an infectious disease doctor fit the bill.

This infection was particularly gnarly. My neck was swollen, my chin was swollen, my tongue was swollen, and I just generally felt awful. My dad drove me to the appointment. I knew what was to come. Two shots of extremely strong antibiotics, one shot in each butt cheek. I had spent my childhood having the same antibiotics prescribed and administered. I'd have to pull my pants down, lean over the exam table, and have two big pokes. Sometimes I'd have multiple rounds in one day, as opposed to driving home and coming back the next day since it was so far away in Northern Virginia. We'd bring books, and I'd have to lie on the waiting room floor for hours between doses because my butt was so sore from the strong medicine in my gluteus maximus. Have I mentioned that my parents are saints?

My dad drove me to this appointment, and we had tried fewer rounds of routine antibiotics with my primary care physician and nothing had been touching this infection in my face, so it was time to tackle it. I was psyching myself up for the two shots (at least) in my butt when the doctor said she would rather give me a larger dose via IV in the office. IVs suck, but one needle was better than two, so I was down with this approach. I thought it would be faster in the long run than waiting for several rounds of butt shots. They took me to another room and hooked me up to the IV. The nurse got it on the first try, which was a miracle in itself, so I was feeling pretty good. Also, I didn't have to have someone touch my butt or stick needles into it, so things were looking up for ole' Han.

They hooked the IV up and started the antibiotic. It was the same exact medicine that I had in the butt shots, so I had been exposed to this medicine literally hundreds of times in my life. Cue the ominous music. I started feeling a little weird, and I told my dad this. He thought I was just trying to get out of having the IV and having to stay at the doctor. I'm pretty sure on the way there, I told him I was feeling 100 percent better and that the appointment was totally not at all needed (as my neck is swollen like three times the size it should have been). He was not fooled by me being a fool. He told me to calm down and just chill and that I was fine. It kind of sucks to be told you're okay as a kid when you don't feel okay, but as a parent, I tell my kids *all the time* that they are okay, so I think it's just what you gotta do.

A few more minutes went by, and I still felt really weird. I told my dad I didn't feel good, and he told me to just relax. It was just because the medicine was going in quickly through the IV. It was probably just a little uncomfortable. I tried to be chill and joke and laugh, but I was feeling really weird. I told him I really didn't feel good, and by that point, he was over my complaining and told me to stop fussing, and it would be over soon. Once more, I impressed upon him that I really didn't feel good and was hot. He still didn't believe me, and so I took my pants off.

Listen, I don't always just take my pants off. It's not my first line of defense in life. But I was really, really hot, and one arm had the IV in it, so taking my shirt off didn't seem like the best choice, so pants it was! Well, I attempted to take my pants off, the best I could do with one hand, as my other arm had the IV in it, and if I've learned anything in life, it is to never disturb a functioning IV. I wasn't starting this whole process all over. So, I was unbuttoning my pants and trying to shimmy out of them all while leaving my one arm with the IV in perfectly still. My dad must have been preoccupied because when he looked over, I had my pants almost to my thighs, and he quickly shouted, asking me what I was doing. His shouting must have alerted a nurse because she came rushing in and saw my legs were covered in hives. She quickly lifted my shirt up and saw that my whole belly was covered with hives too. I was having an allergic reaction! The nurse turned off the IV drip, called the doctor, and they quickly started me on Benadryl.

Turns out it wasn't just an allergic reaction; I was going into anaphylactic shock. Like, the kind that kills you. As you can tell, I didn't die, and when I tell you, I've never felt so vindicated in my life. My poor dad sat there helplessly as the nurse and doctor were pumping me with allergy medicine and whatever else was necessary to stop me from dying. I looked at him and said, "I told you I didn't feel good!" They got me feeling good as new, and I guess the half dose of near-fatal antibiotic did some good because my infection did clear up. Unfortunately, then I had to do all this other allergy testing because, apparently, medicines live in families, and if you're allergic to one of the families, you're probably allergic to all. Who knows why my body decided out of the blue it was allergic to that medicine that day since I'd had it hundreds of times before? I guess my body was tired of butt shots, which I don't blame or fault at all for that nonsense.

My dad was so apologetic, and I think he just absolutely felt horrible. I think he had a cell phone and had let my mom know what was happening (since we had to stay a while for monitoring to ensure that death didn't come back for me). We got home, my mom gave me the biggest hug ever, and we sat on the front porch in the late afternoon sunshine as I recounted to her how I really did tell my dad I didn't feel good before I tried to take my pants off.

My parents never fought in front of us, but I imagine there may have been a little fight that night on account of the whole near-death experience. But all is well, so don't worry, Papa! Who knew I'd do that in the doctor's office that day? Wow, a real shock to all of us. (Get it, shock, because it's anaphylactic shock). The moral of the story is if a girl tells you she doesn't feel good . . . you may want to listen. Unless you can VISIBLY see that she doesn't feel good and she's, in fact, telling you that she's totally fine . . . that's probably a lie to get out of things.

4

Popping Balloons, It's Not a Party

When I was a senior in high school, I got boob implants. Okay, not REALLY, but pretty close. I was preparing emotionally and physically to have the biggest surgery of my life. My entire life, we spent countless hours in doctor's appointments with my plastic surgeon talking about THE BIG ONE. The big surgery would change everything. They were going to totally break my jaw and rebuild my entire face. Casual for a seventeen-year-old, right? Anyway, to prepare my body, they had to stretch my skin and tissue. Gross. To do so, they put balloons filled with saline under my skin in my chest. Aka boob implants . . . but on my collar bone area. Double boobs. Each week I would go to the doctor, and they'd stick a needle in the balloons and fill them more and more with saline. While my friends were getting ready for prom and graduation and making summer plans for their last summer at home before college, I was getting balloons injected with saline-filled up in my chest. I have very small actual boobs, so these balloons quickly overtook my real boob size, but they were up in my armpits and by my chin. As if I wasn't disfigured looking enough . . .

The thought was that they'd stretch my skin out so that when they went to reconstruct my jaw and rebuild it, they wouldn't have to do skin grafts to accommodate the reconfiguration; there would just be extra skin there to make it work, as Tim Gunn would say. My plastic surgeon was brilliant and kept me alive, so I'm not going to say this was a bad idea . . . but also not the best idea he's ever had. When I tell you how painful it is to have literal plastic or silicone, whatever foreign material balloons are, inside you, literally stretching your skin out . . . it is *horrible*. My skin was so bruised and raw from the constant injections. The saline would sting so badly. Every week, I had to go in for these terrible injections. My chest was getting more and more puffy. I had to buy bigger shirts that were loose, to try to hide the ever-growing things inside my chest. My skin was stretched so thin and so sore; we tried cocoa butter and Vitamin E oil.

My friends all knew what was going on. They were the kindest and sweetest bunch of pals a girl could ever ask for when preparing for yet another surgery and undergoing constant pokes and prods instead of focusing on having the best carefree summer of life. We were all hanging out on my patio late one night, talking and laughing underneath the stars. I can remember exactly where I was sitting and that I was sitting across from my friend, Emily. Usually, my parents wouldn't have let friends hang out so late, but I think because of everything else I had going on, my parents let me have a free pass. I got to hang out with friends and not think about all the heavy stuff that a seventeen-year-old shouldn't have to think about.

I was under the night sky and didn't have to worry about how my chest looked under my shirt or if it was awkward looking, not that my friends would have cared anyway, but having the protection of darkness was comforting anyway. We were talking and laughing and had already been told twice by my parents, who were in bed, to be quiet. I started to feel a little wetness in my armpit, but I thought it was just sweat from the early June heat. At one point, I remember feeling really wet in my armpit but didn't feel like it was that hot outside. I touched my armpit with my hand and looked at my fingers in the meek porch light, and my fingers were dark and shiny. I remember saying *Oh my gosh, I'm bleeding* to my friends and running inside.

I'm SURE they were all very bewildered and confused, as you know . . . spontaneously bleeding isn't typical of every teenage girl. I ran inside and went up to my mom and dad's bedroom and said I'M BLEEDING. What I didn't know was that my shirt was soaked in blood. We just couldn't tell outside because the porch light was behind me. Never have I ever been so close to passing out than when I looked down and saw a blood-soaked shirt. One of the balloons had pushed through my skin in my armpit, and essentially, I just had a big open wound.

My mom had me lie down on her bathroom floor and stay very still. I don't remember this, but Emily said my mom came out very calmly and said that I was okay but that they needed to go home right now. I mean, gosh. I must have been very hard to be friends with in my youth, with fake boob implants and blood everywhere. God bless my girlfriends. We were tight with the plastic surgeon, and I think my mom had his home number or at least a nurse's number, so she called and explained the situation. He couldn't do anything for me that night, so my mom legit tried to push the balloon back in and then bandage me right on up. As if I hadn't just been bleeding away the past twenty to thirty minutes, and my dumb butt just thought I was sweaty.

We went to the doctor, and he had to take the tissue/skin expander out. The relief that I have felt getting that demon thing out of me was the best. But, it also meant that potentially the surgery that was coming in a few weeks was going to be more complicated. Ain't nothing ever easy. Sheesh. Then, in a fun turn of events, because I had had a gaping wound in my body, it got infected. Because why not. Why wouldn't my chest get infected after going through a month of hell while the surgeon is attempting to stretch my skin out. Due to the infection in my chest, when I went to have the surgery, they couldn't even use any of the skin or tissue that I had just spent the last 4-5 weeks of my life stretching out! The doctors were still able to reconstruct the bones in my jaw but had to use skin grafts from other parts of me. This was not the first time doctors tried experimental treatments on me without total success.

I'm telling you, I deserved a medal that year. I spent the summer after graduation in a hospital bed in my living room, looking like a zombie. Thus is the story of my sweat-turned-blood, fake-boob-implant adventure. I still have scars on both my armpits from those dang balloons. So, it probably was a good idea in theory, but not a good idea in the reality that, "Hannah's body rarely does what anyone anticipates it will do despite our best efforts otherwise."

Also, because I thought it would be funny, I asked my best high school gal pal, Emily, to write up how she remembers that night. The following essay is by Emily Ball:

Being friends with Hannah is always an adventure. She's either pulling a prank or falling down a manhole or crafting Dolly Parton tchotchkes or reacting to extreme medical emergencies as if they were just a paper cut.

When we were in high school, there was one night when a group of us were sitting on her back porch. I can't remember exactly what we'd gotten up to that day, but in Warrenton, Virginia, there wasn't much to do except sit around and enjoy each other's company - which wasn't a bad activity at all. We were either giggling over boys or contemplating the nuances of grace and the existence of heaven. We were prone to either extreme in those days.

Suddenly, Hannah stood up abruptly. I remember her vaguely touching her armpit, which I thought was sort of funny, but I couldn't see much in the heavy dusk except for her wordlessly moving into the house. None of us were bothered at first. But as more minutes passed, we started feeling uneasy at her unexplained absence. It's hard, when you love Hannah, not to rush to the extreme scenario. While we spent our days wallowing in what was mostly teenage melodrama, Hannah was actually living it - real life or death worry, physical pain, countless surgeries and procedures with risks and fragile promises we could only begin to understand.

At that time, Hannah had balloons (I am not certain of the medical terminology here) inserted under the skin around her armpits. As I recall, the purpose was to stretch her skin enough that they could use it for an upcoming surgery on her neck and jaw (Aside to the author - Hannah, please forgive me if I'm butchering this explanation and getting it all wrong; all I know for certain is that it sounded tortuous, and it truly was).

We all started to let our minds wander to the balloons and the upcoming procedure and the familiar tinge of worry that always hounded us whenever Hannah had something medical approaching; just then, Mrs. Vaughn, Hannah's saintly mother with a voice that feels like a warm hug, opened the door from the kitchen and stepped out onto the porch.

"Well, Hannah's balloon has popped," she said, in the way you might tell someone the time if they asked or read today's headline from the newspaper at the breakfast table. "There's quite a bit of blood, so I think we will need to deal with that, and it'd be best if you all just went home."

I remember the next time I talked to Hannah; she laughed while explaining that she thought she had suddenly started sweating profusely, only to touch her fingers to her armpit and realize she was covered in red.

We all scattered and whispered our worries on the walk down the sloping driveway to our cars. Mrs. Vaughn had seemed so calm - but a balloon popping inside of you did not seem like a chill thing, did it? Later, we'd laugh about this night and how bizarre but also totally ordinary it was if you were Hannah or in Hannah's orbit. Just another night giggling with your pals in the suburbs and confronting an urgent medical crisis in between discussions of who our favorite guy was on Gilmore Girls. That's just how it always was.

The process of thinking back on my life in the context of others is really interesting to me. All these wild things happened to me and I just rolled with it because it was just my life, I didn't know anything else, but hearing my siblings and friends tell stories like this is really eye opening as to how truly wild growing up was for me. I am really grateful that I was, and still am, surrounded by a group of gals who loved me, accepted me, and could laugh through traumatic events with me.

5

The Time I Pooped Outside the Post Office During a Blizzard

Once I lived on the side of a mountain in Colorado in Snowmass. I lived and worked at a Deaf camp, and at one point, there were fifteen people living in the house I lived in. One-third of these people were deaf, and the rest of us were hearing. Half of us worked at the Deaf camp, and half were ski instructors that worked elsewhere and partied a lot. I hung out with the boys who were ski instructors. They were my best friends, the most fun, and so wild. We all keep in touch and talk fondly about that winter and spring together. By the time I had moved out, they had all moved out, too, and some of the magic was lost, but it was the best and worst eight months of my life.

Anyway, the camp had a nurse named Chelsea who would frequently come on the weekends to assist while campers were there. Chelsea was my saving grace, my best friend, and the funniest person ever. She is who got me through those horrible eight months, and we'd count down the days until she'd come back to the camp the next weekend. Oh my gosh, she was the best. She's still alive, so she's probably still the best; we just aren't as close. Anyway, I sometimes have little ulcers on my colon that make me poop blood. I actually have no idea why this happens or how, but it was also the first time I was ever on my own and on the other side of the country from literally anyone and everyone I had ever known so . . . I didn't heed much caution to my bloody poops. They had gotten significantly worse one month, and I was in really bad stomach pain all the time and just pooping blood. Turns out this is not a good thing for your body to do. Chelsea was at camp, and we were in full camper mode, activities, games, bonfires, all the things. I had told my boss, Lisa, that I had been having this festive issue in the bathroom, and she was pretty concerned for me, but I had a job to do (this was before I realized every employee is replicable and rarely should you ever go above and beyond for any job ever), and I was soldiering on.

Chelsea and I had finished doing dishes after supper one night, and it was snowing because it was winter in Colorado, and I was like, "I think I really need to actually see a doctor." It was a Friday night, and did I mention we lived on the side of a mountain? So, Chelsea, as best friend and nurse, was like, "I'll drive you; let's party." So, we got in her car and drove down the side of the mountain in a snowstorm and made it to the main road. We made it 30 minutes to the hospital in Aspen and got there probably around 9pm.

We got to the ER, and the doors were locked. Like legit locked. Lights off. We were like, ummm this is a hospital, so we found a doorbell and rang it and rang it until someone finally answered. My angel from above, Frank. He told us we were at the wrong entrance and needed to drive around. We finally got to the right door that was unlocked and lit up. Frank had a gown ready for me in a triage room, so I changed quickly. I really had to use the bathroom, though, after this long journey, so I walked out to the empty ER and called for Frank. I told him I really needed to use the bathroom, and he told me I couldn't yet because they hadn't checked me in. I was like, dude, believe me, I have to go now. So, I was standing in the hallway arguing with Frank, and then I just had a little accident on the ER floor.

Let me note here: Brandon is convinced that every adult has pooped their pants at one point in life. I maintain that as an adult, I never have. Because I haven't. He knows this story, though, and throws it in my face, but I had no pants on. I only had a hospital gown that opened in the back, aka when I had a little accident on the ER floor, there were no pants for it to fall into. There was just air and the floor.

Frank was shocked and appalled, and I literally said, "I told you I had to use the bathroom!" You'd think that was the worst thing to happen, but oh no, it got worse. Frank apparently was also the janitor in this one-man show of an ER, so after he cleaned up after me, he came back to actually check me in. Luckily, he didn't have too many questions to ask since he had seen my ailment in action several minutes prior. Meanwhile, Chelsea took this all in stride like a champ as her friend pooped on the floor. Frank said we needed to do lots of blood tests. Cool.

This is a good time to mention that my veins pretty much do not exist. Like even on a good day. I have to tell anyone drawing my blood to use the tiniest needle they have and to get the baby or cancer doctors because as good of a nurse as you are, you probably won't get my blood. Recently I had my blood drawn for a life insurance policy, and she finally got some to come out into the tube, *and it went back in.* She said wow, I have never seen that happen before. My body is so resistant to giving blood, it literally took it back from a needle. Hand to God that is true.

So, Frank was like we gotta get some blood; let's rock and roll. I told Frank good luck because you know . . . pooping your brains out kinda dehydrates you. So, Frank tried three times and then filled some gloves with hot water and made me sit on the table with hot water-filled gloves all up and down my arms to try to warm my veins. Warmth is the way to my heart, so he wasn't wrong. In the meantime, he gave me his personal iPad to watch YouTube videos. We watched the video of the "Honey Badger Who Don't Give a F" (I just rewatched this as I'm writing, and dang, it's so funny). It was around 11 p.m., and no one else had come to the ER (probably because they, too, went to the locked door and Frank was too busy cleaning up my accident to answer the doorbell), and Chelsea, Frank, and I were fast best friends. We were just cackling, chatting it up, sharing YouTube videos, and hoping my veins would warm up.

Finally, after *seven* pokes, Frank got some blood from me. No idea what the results were, but I had to see a GI doctor and have a colonoscopy at age twenty-one. Chelsea and I finally left the ER with no answers at like midnight and came outside to another two to three inches of snow on the ground. Chelsea didn't have a snow scraper, so we were outside at midnight after four hours in the ER scraping snow and ice off her windshield with expired library cards. We headed back to the camp, and we got to the turn to go back up the mountain to the camp. I was suddenly struck with a rumbly tumbly (stomach) and said, "Chels . . . I'm not going to make it!" She was like "It's midnight; we can't do anything; just hold it." There was no holding it. There was nothing nearby except the post office. Chelsea pulled into the parking lot, and I went behind the building (there are no trees!), and unpleasant things occurred. Also, having your butt out in like literal 0-degree weather is not at all fun. I finished up, piled snow on top of my junk, and we went back up the mountain to camp.

Like, what an insane story. I don't know how these things happen to me. Turns out ibuprofen makes my colon ulcers mad, so I can't take it anymore. Also, when I saw the GI doctor, she offered me a medical marijuana card (it had *just* become legal in Colorado for medical reasons) without me even telling her what was wrong. I stupidly told her I didn't need that. (Don't worry, I smoked a lot recreationally to find out if it would heal me.) All the boys I lived with were mad at me for not getting a medical card essentially for free since it was just offered to me. All is well, and Chelsea is the real MVP for putting up with a disgusting friend and driving my broken butt around in a snowstorm on a Friday night. If that ain't love, I don't know what love is.

6

My Body Remembers It All

Recently, I had my first mammogram. This doesn't sound too odd until I share with you that I was thirty years old and that it was diagnostic. The literal results from the mammogram were fine. No issues, no scariness, just some dense tissue and calcium deposits. However, the physical results were still lingering two weeks later. I don't think it's normal to break out in a rash after having a mammogram, but welcome to today's episode of *My Body Doing Weird Things*. We are in our 30th season, and this is episode twenty-four for the year, right before the year ends. My trauma rash has dissipated, but part of me fears my left boob may never be the same.

I'm no stranger to medical procedures. I've had over

fifty surgeries in my short time on earth, and the number of procedures I've had is in the hundreds. The number of blood draws, needle sticks, and times I've heard, "Oops, I'll try again," is in the thousands. My body remembers them all.

I can remember being very little and arriving at the hospital in the wee hours of the morning, before they even turned on all the waiting room lights, stomach growling for food since my last meal was the night before. I played with the same hospital toys year after year as I was constantly going back for more procedures. I remember the slight itch of hospital gowns that were made for children, but somehow were always too big for my small frame. I remember the *Lion King* poster hung on the right wall of the lab, where I would stare into Simba and Nala's eyes as nurses and phlebotomists squeezed, poked, prodded, and coaxed my practically non-existent veins into coming to the surface, only to roll away the minute the needle was inserted.

Once, I read that a leading factor of PTSD is having surgery as a child. I used to joke that a trauma-informed therapist would have a field day with my extensive medical history. On any given day, I can close my eyes and fully taste, smell, and feel exactly how it feels lying on the operating room table with anesthesia hooked up to me and being told to count backwards from ten. Even writing this, I got clammy and claustrophobic and had to take a break. My body remembers it all. Memories are like file folders, there for me to flip through and remember each procedure, every bit of dental work, failed blood draw attempt, each painstaking surgery and procedure tucked away in a cold, sterile cabinet.

I expected mammograms to be uncomfortable, but no one told me they would be traumatizing. I sincerely hope this isn't everyone's experience because I think if every person had the experience I did, we'd surely find another way by now. The techs tried their best, but given my small boobs, she didn't have much to work with! The first tech was so sweet and tried her hardest to contort me into the machine, apologizing all the while, so I did whatever I was asked to do. I figured out a very long time ago that being quiet and submissive during medical procedures typically made them go faster.

So, I turned my body into moldable clay and became quieter as she kept trying to reposition me in the cold machine. She couldn't get the needed images, so she called in another tech. Together they pushed my face against the metal, lifted, pulled, and smashed my chest between the plates, and I only grew quieter. The apologies that flowed copiously from their lips were no match for the humiliation and pain that was radiating within me. I could feel my body growing hot with anger and tears at the tech's frustrated sigh. What was supposed to be a routine procedure was becoming another file in my cabinet of medical trauma.

I grew hotter and more humiliated with every minute as they sighed with frustration that my body wouldn't bend and fold and contort how they needed it to. I was sure this was a routine procedure, but once again, My Body Does

Weird Things, and I couldn't even get my boobs smashed correctly. By the time a third tech came in for backup, I was crying. I wasn't sure if it was out of frustration, pain, or anger. Probably a combination of all three. I stood there with tears streaming down my face unable to talk, only nod and follow directions the nurses gave me. They were sympathetic, but had a job to do and I'm sure I was making them run behind schedule. I tried to make my body as moldable and movable as I could so they could press and smash my body to obtain the scan.

Quickly, I started dissociating. This term is new to me, but the feelings are not. The term finally put language to feelings I've felt since I was a toddler. I didn't know that my quietness and inward shrinking and disconnected thoughts had a word, but I am so glad they do. I could feel every pull, push, and turn of the mammogram machine. I was fading away, just as I had faded away several years ago when five of my front teeth got ripped out in one day and the oral surgeon simply said, "oops", and just as I had more recently when I was being wheeled back to the operating room only to have the anesthesiologist put the brakes on my hospital bed and tell me he couldn't do the surgery to remove my spleen. What I've been learning is that I've been dissociating in the presence of medical professionals for thirty years, but somehow my body still remembers it all.

I came home after my mammogram and took a hot shower and cried. It was hard to explain to my husband how horrible the appointment was. I was frustrated that he seemed to only care that the results were benign. No cancer, no diseases, no new diagnosis. But I couldn't explain the horrific experience I had endured. When I got out of the shower, we discovered a bright red angry rash on my boob, so he drew a circle around it to make sure it didn't get bigger, then drew a smiley face inside the circle, so at least the angry red rash was smiling. He bought me all the creams and lotions we could think to try, but this little trauma rash was stubborn.

Eventually the rash faded, but the trauma didn't. I never expected that a simple mammogram would bring up thirty years of feelings, emotions, and trauma. My life is busier now than ever with working, raising four boys into men, running a business, and fighting to be heard every day. Honestly, it doesn't feel like I have time for these emotions, but Lord knows I don't want to wait another thirty years to deal with them. If I had never heard a friend talk about dissociation on Instagram, I would never have words for these feelings. I'm always so appreciative of those who go first and share hard things, so I hope this essay can give words and emotions to others too. Clearly, I still have a lot of work to do on dealing with my feelings and medical trauma; I may drag my feet to do it, but I am hopeful that I will continue and I know it will be worth it. I'm also hopeful that ten years from now when I have to have my next mammogram, it'll be less traumatizing

Part II
Loving People and Animals

7

Dating Confessions

When I was a freshman in college, I had my first boyfriend. Late bloomer, ya know? Also, he was visually impaired. Which, if you're a mean person and a hater, you'd be not surprised that he couldn't fully see what I looked like—jokes on you; he had peripheral vision—but I don't think you're a mean person because you're reading my book, so thanks!

He was so sweet, such a kind dude, loved NASCAR and country music (did I mention I went to school in the mountains of North Carolina?), and he was *crazy* about me. I was so lucky to have my first boyfriend be so great. My friends liked him; he was beloved by all on campus, he was down for adventures that were potentially unsafe for a visually impaired person to be going on, and he knew how to have fun. I had never had a boyfriend before, and I fell hard for him. This was around 2008-2009, and boy, do my Facebook memories remind me of how much I liked this dude.

The same time we were dating, we were involved in several campus clubs and activities, and at one point, one of the club leaders asked me to grab lunch. He was older and married, and I surely thought I was in trouble. He sat me down and was like, "Hey, I'm so glad you're dating Tim (name changed), but I'm a bit worried." Gasp! He asked me what I liked about Tim, and I told him lots of things that ultimately were pretty surface level. He agreed that all those things were great things, but he said, "Hannah, I know you have big dreams and goals and a big personality, and I really care for you and Tim, but I don't think you're on the same level." I immediately got defensive and mad. How dare someone try to speak into my relationship, much less the first relationship I was ever in. I went on to defend the boy and say, but he's going to do XYZ, he hopes XYZ, and I can see XYZ happening!

Then he said something that has changed my life and that I have since gone on to say to countless friends when asked for dating advice. "You can't date potential." Well, woof. What a shot to the heart. He went on to tell young Hannah that Tim was a great dude and that he could make her happy, but if she wanted whatever she wanted in life and Tim was on a different path, she couldn't hope or pray that he would eventually catch up. The two paths weren't wrong, but she couldn't spend months or years of her life hoping any partner would grow into the potential that she saw in them.

Man—I was pissed. Yes, I'm an optimist, and I think I can see the good in almost all people and situations, but deep down, I knew he was right. It's so easy when we date someone, especially when experiencing young, dumb love, to see the potential that *we* want them to grow into. We think, "If only he would do XYZ, he would be perfect." But that's us being controlling, not loving them for who they are where they are. He continued on saying that I could continue to date him, of course, and ultimately hope that he'd change and step up to what I needed and wanted him to be, or I could let go because it didn't appear that we were growing and changing at the same pace. The boyfriend did nothing wrong, and who he was and where he was, ultimately, was totally fine; it just wasn't what I needed.

I spent the next week in turmoil, and it was very dramatic. I would go lie on the back soccer fields on campus, where no one ever went, and journal and cry. I have journals from that time, but they are too cringey to even read. I concluded that same week, after incessant conversations with my friends (thanks, pals), that I was really in love with *having* a boyfriend but not in love *with him*. He was 110 percent in love with me. I was his first girlfriend, and he was sold on picking out our future kids' names and moving back to his hometown and living a small and comfortable life. I was really sad. This boy had done nothing but love, care, and dote upon me for months on end. People knew us on campus as a couple, and I really liked his friends and his dormmates and didn't want to have to break up with all of them too.

My memory is fuzzy, but I do think that along the way, I had told him about my lunch conversation and had asked him to show me that he could live up to his potential. Potential he wanted for himself and that I wanted for him. He shared big dreams with me but wasn't taking any steps to put those dreams into action. I knew I needed to end the relationship, despite not wanting to.

Confession: I liked having a boyfriend. I liked meeting up between classes; I liked making out with him; I liked having a boy to steal sweatshirts from—you know, all the typical first-love kind of things. He also gave me hope that another boy someday would like me. Up until then, I really wasn't sure. He made me feel so assured and taken care of and loved, not despite my medical stuff, but alongside it. There wasn't a ton he could physically do for me with his eyesight, but there was a lot I could do for him, and so another gross truth: It was nice to feel needed. This was the first relationship I was in where I felt needed, and I enjoyed that, but this was certainly not the last. Feeling needed goes hand in hand with seeing potential in people; I don't think it's a bad thing. I appreciate these qualities about myself, but it can be really hard not to get those things confused with healthy partnerships.

One evening I went to his dorm room to break up with him. He wasn't expecting me, but I called him and told him I was outside (he lived on the first floor), and he came and let me in. He could tell I was upset, but I wasn't crying. I had never broken up with someone before! I practiced with my dormmates before going over to his dorm. We sat on his bed where we had sat daily for the past six months doing homework, talking, watching movies, making out, or playing games. I figured quick was the best strategy, so without much chit-chat, I came out and said I think we needed to break up. As I said, he knew how I had been feeling prior to that night, but he did not think this would be the outcome. He was shocked. That made it *way* harder. He immediately burst into tears and grabbed onto me as if physically holding onto me meant he could emotionally hold on to me too. He begged me to reconsider and asked what he could do to change my mind. There was a pregnant pause, and then I stood up from the bed and told him I was sorry again and that I was leaving.

I got back to my dorm and realized I didn't have my keycard or my phone to get in the dorm. I must have left them on his bed—guys—this is the last thing I wanted to happen. I walked across the quad and knocked on his window since it was on the first floor, and when he opened it, he was still crying, and he said, "Oh my gosh, Hannah did you change your mind and want to get back together?" Sheepishly I said, "No, I left my phone on your bed." I can't even explain the range of emotions his face showed in those moments. Complete elation, hope, confusion, heartbreak all in a two-second span. He got my phone off his bed and tossed it to me out the window, and I apologized again and scurried back to my dorm.

I felt so bad. Clearly, I didn't plan to leave my stuff there or to re-break his heart after breaking it less than ten minutes prior. However, thirteen years later, I think this is a really funny story. It's not funny that I hurt his feelings or completely crushed him, none of that was intentional, and that's what happens during breakups, but it was the most honest and accidental mistake that I had ever made in my whole life. I hope you can laugh with me about it all while appreciating how mortifying my life really is sometimes.

8

My Love Story
(Also, the Death of Patrick Henry
the Hedgehog)

I had no intention of ever writing about my "love story." In fact, Brandon was probably not going to be in the book at all except to share funny anecdotes about insane things I did that he had to deal with (I mean, experience, and appreciate). But then my author coach (shout out to Andrea!) told me most people enjoy a great love story AND that people would be interested in reading mine (insert eye roll). This is *my* story dang it; Brandon is too cool to talk about because he will outshine me. But I reckon if the people want it . . . here we go!

Actually, let me backup . . . I *never* thought I'd get married—like never. I can show you text receipts from my college years to my mid 20s where I never thought it was for me. I sat down in my college coffee shop one day and legitimately *wailed* to my pastor that I wanted a boyfriend so badly, and it was never going to happen. I was a peach to be around. I swear, I never thought someone would fall in love with me and want to marry me.. I started dreaming bigger and wanting more things out of life and just felt like those things would and could happen without a partner in life and I wasn't going to let it stop me. After college I moved to Colorado on my own, then two years later, I moved to Brazil on my own. I never let the lack of a relationship stop me from chasing wild things, seeking adventure, and choosing joy.

Once a boy in college told me, "You're everything I've ever wanted in a wife, but I'm not attracted to you because you're not attractive." That's just how I assumed the rest of my life would go. Luckily, "Mean" by Taylor Swift came out at almost this exact same time, so I would just drive past his house screaming the lyrics and blasting that song with my girlfriends. I don't think I was lacking confidence in myself that I wasn't—fill-in-the-blank— whatever someone wanted in a partner. I was just resolved that it wasn't going to happen. I dated in and after college and while I was in grad school. I had a lot of fun with the "insta" dopamine hits, and then things would fizzle out. Even when I met Brandon, I still never thought he'd be my future husband, and he *for sure* did not think I'd be his future wife. At the time he was anti-marriage and pretty sure he would never get married. But all my charm, wit, funniness, and love won him over.

Brandon and I met on Tinder January 28, 2016. We messaged back and forth for a while. Then, I told him he had to either ask for my number or stop messaging me because I didn't like spending time texting on Tinder.

He obliged and asked for my number, and then we started texting and made plans for the following Saturday evening after I went to a wedding. He was staying at his best friend's house in Richmond (sometime during that week, I found out he actually lived two hours away), and we planned to meet there. He took me inside and introduced me to his best friends, and then we went upstairs to talk, and by talk, I mean make out—then we talked. At the time Patrick Henry, my hedgehog, was actively dying. He was only like a year old; it wasn't my fault! I told Brandon all about Patrick Henry and his active dying-ness and then I *started to cry*. I mean, who the frick cries on a first date over a dying hedgehog? Brandon was nice about it though, so that was positive. Somewhere mid-conversation, Brandon asked me to be his girlfriend, and I said no considering I had just met him for the first time. We continued to see each other on the weekends, and on March 1st, I sent an email to some best friends and said,

But he's really great. He's got the strongest country accent I've ever heard. It's good. This man might change my life. I've been really guarded and scared

honestly. I usually move fast, and I'm like, "let's date, let's be official," whatever blah blah, but I've been really guarded, and I think a lot of that has to do with being so hurt by—insert ex-boyfriend's name here—in December. That was the first time I really got my heart broken, and it sucked, and I don't want to do that again, so I am taking it slow. Brandon is really patient and kind and is such a words-of-affirmation-kind of dude, and I think I had written him off as kinda a country dude. The conversations we started to have been about everything: religion, politics, life; I was pleasantly surprised he was way more thoughtful than I knew, and it's awesome. We will see. But it's cool that God is using Brandon to remind me how loved and enjoyed I am by the Lord, and I think God is using me in Brandon's life as well. I have no idea what will happen but right now it is good and exciting.

Brandon asked me several times over the next month to be his girlfriend, and I said no until March 17. I finally acquiesced, and ten months into dating, I told him I loved him before I left his house to come back to Richmond after a weekend together. He said, "I think I love you too," to which I said, "*You think?* What percentage?!" and he said 96 percent. On our wedding day, I asked him if it was finally 100 percent, and he said 99.9 percent. I just asked him again nearly six years after we first met, and he said it was 100 percent finally. Whew.

We got engaged the day after our one-year dating

anniversary, and he moved to Richmond soon after that. We lived in the 900 square foot house I had been living in with roommates for the past year, and he brought the real love of his life, Suri, the three-legged Pitbull with him. We had a really fun time finally not being long distance and working and enjoying life in the city together. We got married in September of 2017 with our besties by our sides and then bought our first house in the spring of 2018. When I think back to the scared girl who wrote that email to her best friends in March 2016 from her computer in an intern office in grad school, I cannot believe we've made it this far.

When people ask me what I love about Brandon, the first thing I always say is that he's never made me feel insecure. Not once in six years. With other dudes I had dated (and there were lots of losers, so don't judge me too hard), I had felt insecure about how I looked or sounded or like I was never enough or that they never really knew or loved me. From the day we started chatting, Brandon made me feel seen and understood, and we talked about how I looked that first day, and he never batted his eyes twice about it. He wasn't concerned about what others thought; he always just focused on if I was okay. Brandon is so confident in who he is and what he likes and cares about, including me. I remember my mom telling me that early on, "Hannah, he's just so self-assured. Not in an arrogant way, but in a comfortable way that puts you at ease, too." He's happy to have his mind changed (and dang has he changed his mind on things in six years) and isn't pushy about anything. He makes me laugh every day. He's a better dad than I am mom. I remember sitting in class one day texting him about what we both wanted as far as kids. We were still just barely dating and talking about kids. I told him I wanted to foster and adopt some day, and he thought that sounded great. He literally didn't bat an eye again. Now here we are. Six years in. Two houses bought; one house sold. Four kids. Two trips to Mexico. Countless concerts, car rides, laughs, and tears shared. We feel totally incredulous about everything in our life. We had no idea any of this would happen and are just excited to see what happens next.

I've already allied myself with the fact that I'm not a perfect partner all the time. I can be bossy and determined and can move faster than tornado speed, and Brandon is left just gaping at what happened. On a whim, in April 2020, I said what if we moved to the country? He said, oh yeah that would be cool someday. Three months later, we bought our farmhouse. I can move one hundred miles an hour, and he can move about three, but by the time I've gone in a full circle, he's digested what I've said the first time and can talk some sense into me. He's rational and calm and logical. I'm fast, emotional, and tenacious. Remember, I'm a rebel. I also rebel against the ideas that things have to *always* be thought out and planned.

For the record, I don't ever rebel against Brandon. I respect him and have grown to learn that his patience with things and my insane ideas far outweigh the potential benefits I think exist. Just this week, I tried to convince him we should buy our friend's tiny house, school bus. Initially, he was like yeah that would be so fun. Then I went deep into the research and dreaming of ideas and thinking about all we could do with it. Then we sat down and had a state of the union where we actually talk about things not just in a fantastical way, and his logic often outweighs my passion. Turns out, we probably don't need a school bus in our backyard to be a mobile plant store, elderberry bus, bachelorette pad, or any of the other ideas I had ready to pitch him, Shark Tank style. He's right, but I was sad.

When we met, Brandon wouldn't say he was the kind of person to dream big dreams. He was happy to be with his people and make money and get by in life. I never needed him to be different than that. He is so faithful and loyal and just absolutely the best. I have hoped and tried to change boyfriends in the past, and to be honest, friends too. I can be bossy, I told you. But I never wanted him to change. He accepted me so fully, and I returned the favor. I encouraged him to dream big and see his own potential, and he did. He's doing things he loves with his life and killing it and makes supper every night because I don't cook. I saw a text my mom sent him a few months ago that said how much she loved him and how he is the perfect husband for me and how grateful she was for him in my life. The feeling is quite mutual, Mama. He's the bomb.

Brandon and I hope to inspire people to have an intentional relationship. Our relationship itself is not inspirational. We support each other's dreams, big or small. When he finished one associate degree in mechanical engineering and then immediately said he wanted to study horticulture and get another degree, I said here you go, baby, and handed him some gardening gloves. We hang out together a lot without the kids. He is slowly teaching me to cook after a million years of not knowing how. He helps pull my jeans down when I have to pee right after I paint my nails. I rub his back every night before bed. We take trips together (thanks grandparents for watching our kids!). We talk about every decision and every dollar. At any moment, one of us can say "spicy salmon roll!" and the other will do the Unagi sign that Ross did on Friends. I got him to try ziplining through the Mayan jungle, and he gets me to watch Cheers with him before bed. None of this is magical or special, but it is intentional. Neither of us married up; we married together, and it's in the top three best things we've ever done. You know the cliché, choose each other every day. It's true. We love choosing each other and choosing decisions that serve us and our family well. We are fiercely protective of our marriage, and I hope we always are. We always joke that he'll die before I will, and I'll get to live out my epic Golden Girls fantasy. Until then, I'm gonna love the crap out of my husband.

9

It's Normal to Have Breakdowns at the Pediatrician's Office, Right?

Recently I took my kid to the pediatrician's office for the first time. We've been so lucky to have really healthy kids. We also have kids that smash their knees on chicken gates and have to go to urgent care, but not kids that get sick and have to go to the pediatrician—which is definitely a plus! We've been to specialists, therapists, psychologists, have had evaluations, and IEP meetings—more times than I wish—but I had never been to a pediatrician's office before as a mama. I spent so much time in specialists' offices as a kid that I don't even remember my own pediatrician. I was much more familiar with my plastic surgeon than any of my regular doctors as a kid.

We found the office, nodded at each other, and went in. We were greeted with a mural of flowers and mirrors and a smiling receptionist in a superhero mask. I finally have a real insurance card for my son, instead of a copy of a copy. I was completely taken aback by the décor. As a new parent, I was unfamiliar with inspirational kid art, which isn't too far off from the Live Laugh Love inspirational art for adults, but more colorful! I didn't know this was an art genre, but now I do—and it's cute. When we walked into that flower-filled office, I didn't anticipate crying, but alas, that was one of the outcomes. The other outcome was that my kid and I split a blue raspberry Slurpee on the way home because he got a shot and because I needed a Slurpee to soothe my soul.

The visit started off on a high note. I had to fill out tons of paperwork; this wouldn't normally be very fun to do, but on the form, it asked for Mother's name, and for the first time in my life, I got to put my name there. I didn't have to put his birth mother's name, I didn't have to put his Department of Social Services Case Worker's name, I didn't have to put his foster care agency worker's name, I got to put my name, and it was legitimate. It wasn't just who he was with that day.

The adoption process took fourteen months. This was after he had already been in our house for six months. I've signed a lot of things before on his behalf: trampoline park waivers, summer camp forms, Boy Scout forms, all things that I could legally sign without any repercussions, but I've never been able to sign school or medical forms. Besides signing the adoption papers with a judge and one social media post, this was the first public declaration of my parenthood.

As an adoptive parent, I spend literally all day every day parenting these kids, but when they are in foster care, you're still never seen as their parents. You have to ask permission to get their hair cut, to let them go to summer camp, and to take them on vacation. It always made me feel less than an adult. I was parenting a kid that I clothed and fed and provided shelter and unyielding love for, but I couldn't sign papers for him. To be able to sign papers in that office as his mother without any disclaimers and without the weight or stigma of foster care or adoption felt so freeing. I was so grateful. I took a picture and shed a little tear of gratitude. He was my boy. I was his mama. Adoption doesn't come without heartache and loss, and I'm not denying that or pretending those things aren't true, but it felt really dang good to be that boy's mama on paper and in that office. My smart, gentle, compassionate boy. I was so proud. I'm sure he was unaware of what was going on inside my heart as I smiled like an idiot behind my mask at him, our relationship and love, and how far we'd come in those two years. Even writing this, I'm so grateful.

All I want in life is for our family and our kids to *just be kids*. I don't want to walk into spaces and explain they are in foster care. I don't want to label myself as an *adoptive* mama everywhere I go. I want to just write Hannah Setzer on the mother line on forms and sign away like any other mom would. Who cares that he has blonde hair and I have brown hair? Who cares that he's already taller than me at age fifteen? But, on this one little form, for just a minute, I got to be an absolutely plain mama.

The visit went on and turned very hard fast. There were many questions about family and medical history that we didn't know the answers to, and while the nurse and doctors were very compassionate, I felt very embarrassed that I couldn't give a full detailed medical history of my son, because we simply were not given or told everything when he first came into our home. I hated that my emotions were on such a roller coaster. He's so kind and gentle and never raised an eyebrow at any of this. He took it all in stride. Again, this may be because he's a kid and doesn't care, or because he's had fifteen years of probing, and well-meaning adults are way too invasive about his life. I hate it all either way for him.

He had to get a vaccine, and he was brave, and I closed my eyes because I couldn't watch it. He asked me why I closed my eyes, and we laughed about how I'm a baby and can't watch and have to have the nurse count one, two, three before sticking any needle in me. He then proceeded to tell me he was braver than I am, which I quickly acquiesced to. We had to sit and wait to make sure he didn't die after his vaccine, so we just talked and laughed. He was easy breezy, and no one would have ever known the wild ride my emotions (his much less) had just been on. We checked out, he was stoked about his new Superman Band-Aid, and we drove down the road to the gas station to get Slurpees. All shots require Slurpees. My entire childhood, my dad would always take me to get a Slurpee after any doctor's appointments. We rode home with the windows down doing cheers with our Slurpee cups with every sip.

We got home and his brothers swarmed him with questions about the Band-Aid and the Slurpee. Kids are really nosy, y'all. For some reason we did a group hug in the driveway, but one brother was in the house, so we tried to walk in a huddle to him, but I had sandals on, and after the fourth time of some boy stomping on my toes, I was over that nonsense. We came inside and found him, and on the count of three we hugged the mess out of him. We are a weird bunch. I'm so grateful for my weirdos and also grateful that I have the most resilient kids. I know I missed out on twelve and a half years of this kid's life, and I am sure I only know half of what he's experienced to make him this resilient.

Foster care is so wild. We adopted four teenage boys, and now I'm crying at pediatricians' offices. Adoption is so beautiful and harsh and unexpected and uncommon. My hope is that we can continue to grow and learn and that we stop assuming how families are knit together. Brandon and I are white, and all our kids are as well, so we don't get the immediate assumptions that many other adoptive families do. All our kids have blonde or brown hair and freckles like Brandon and me. Our kids adopt things we say, like "pitter patter get atter" (from *Letterkenny* of course) and ask us too many questions a day. Oftentimes when I'm in the car with kids— whether one or four—and they are asking me questions and chattering, I get struck by the thoughts of

"*How did this happen to me? How am I so natural with all this?*" I'm not at all saying I'm "World's Best Mama," but on average, I think for becoming a mom at twenty-eight and going from no kids to fostering a total of six in two years, and eventually adopting four of them, I'm doing alright. I'm really grateful for kids that let me figure out how to be a mama while they figure out how to be kids (sometimes for the first time in their lives) right alongside me.

10

Chicken Lizzo & Other Animal Tales

I accidentally have a lot of animals. I'm an animal lover, in a fun aunt kind of way. Growing up, we had cats and various dogs, but I never felt supremely attached. Sure, I love a dog snuggle or a cat curled up in my lap as much as the next gal, but I never felt the need to have my own animals. I'm a pretty autonomous person and very content with taking care of myself and not being responsible for other things.

Then, Patrick Henry happened. I bought a cute young hedgehog and named him Patrick Henry. To be honest, the cool factor of saying I had a hedgehog was more appealing than actually owning a pet. Also, I was single and ready to mingle and figured a hedgehog would help my dating profile. He had a way of bringing people together. Ultimately, perhaps Brandon swiped right on me on Tinder BECAUSE he saw Patrick Henry and then asked me to be his girlfriend as Patrick Henry was dying and I was crying, so really, maybe Patrick Henry's purpose in life was to bring Brandon and I together! Wow, what a guy.

When he died, the vet gave his little body back to me; he was wrapped up like a burrito, and I put him in the freezer until I could get him to my parents' house to be buried, and once, my brother thought it was a burrito and took him out of the freezer and unwrapped him and was horrified to find a frozen Patrick Henry, not a microwavable burrito. Sorry brother.

A year after we started dating, Brandon moved in with me, and Brandon came with a dog. I loved him and wanted to live with my fiancé, so I reckoned I had to accept having a dog, but I wasn't stoked about it. Suri is a three-legged Pitbull Brandon found on the side of the road in a snowstorm. We convinced ourselves that Suri needed a friend, since at his parents' house, they had other dogs. So, soon after Brandon moved in, we adopted another dog that looked just like Suri but had four legs. Riley is the sweetest and was immediately obsessed with Suri and is a complete weirdo. She refuses to eat anywhere except the living room, is scared of her own shadow, and throws up if you try to play peek-a-boo with her. She runs and jumps like a deer and loves her morning zoomies after she poops. The dogs needed a kitten, so we went to the shelter and chose Pete the cat solely on the fact that Brandon thought he had crazy eyes.

Brandon's grandma feeds like twenty wild cats at all times on her back porch and always has kittens. Naturally, I always want all of them and have been known to try to smuggle some home with me every time we visit her. One fall, her wild cats had kittens, and a dwarf Maine Coon kitten named Meatball was born. I met Meatball pretty early in his life and was obsessed. I mean, this kitten was the cutest kitten to ever live. He had a giant head, a very tiny body. and a huge Maine Coon tail. Eeeeek! I love him so much. I had begged Brandon to let me bring him home, and Brandon adamantly said no. Like, he was quite firm in his no. But then one day Brandon's grandma called us and said that she had a tray of cat food she was carrying outside, and I quote, "That damn devil cat tripped me and made me fall; he has to go"! The devil cat she referred to was Meatball. By fall, she meant she fell into a cast iron gate and smashed her face. Ding ding ding! My time to shine. I had to rescue Meatball from whatever fate may have befallen him.

I was having surgery to get my spleen taken out the next day, which was clearly the best time to get a kitten. Brandon's mom brought him, and Pete hated him instantly. I was too busy with having organs taken out of me to care, but they figured themselves out quickly. Meatball was ours, and his head was so big that when he'd lean over to drink water, he would fall into his water bowl because he was so top heavy. He was, and is, so perfect. Sometimes I literally cry because I love him so much. I never knew I'd be so attached to an animal.

Two cats, two dogs, and a hedgehog seemed like a lot of animals for someone who didn't really like animals. They all got along and were bringing us lots of joy, and the addition of Meatball meant Pete stopped biting my calves when he was hungry and bit Meatball instead, and that seemed like enough of a tradeoff for scooping litter boxes. Meanwhile, Brandon and I had talked and dreamed about having backyard chickens someday. Keyword—someday. We had begun our foster care journey by this point and were enjoying life as a family of three. One afternoon, a woman in a local neighborhood group posted a chicken coop and six chickens for sale for $175. I messaged her right away and begged her to let me pay her to have them. I hadn't quite asked Brandon yet (as if you didn't already know I was a bit rebellious!) but I figured I could work on him later. She lived close to us, we had a truck, so I figured it was a no-brainer. Six hens were the most you could have where we lived, and I thought what could literally be better. She didn't message me back for a long time, and I was legitimately devastated that we missed out on them.

By a miracle from above, she messaged me the next day and said if we could pick them up the upcoming weekend, they were ours. We rallied some kind friends and a U-Haul and got the coop and the six gals to our house. I named them all after female hip hop artists: Lizzo, Lil' Kim, Missy Elliott, Eve, Janet Jackson, and Rihanna. We were obsessed with getting eggs and chasing chickens around the backyard. I secretly felt so "crunchy granola" and loved talking about our chickens.

COVID hit, and we bought our farm. By farm, I mean 2.5 acres in the next county over, but trust me, it is paradise and much more farm than our last house in a neighborhood was. We moved our six hennies with us, upgraded to a chicken house, built a fence and we were ready to rock and roll. Quickly, we got more and more chickens, going from about six to twenty in a few weeks. One Saturday, Brandon and I were sitting at a farmer's market, and I was scrolling on Facebook and saw someone had mini piglets listed for sale. You know that immediately, I had to ask Brandon if I could have a mini pig. Surprising to us all, Brandon said yes and we brought home Barry the not so mini mini pig. He immediately loved the chickens waits for them to gather in an area, then charges at them in a game we refer to as, Bowling for Chickens. Facebook posts hit me again in the fall of 2022, and someone posted a tiny orange kitten up for adoption. They had found him at the pumpkin patch, but he wasn't getting along with their dog and toddler. I picked him up that night and let Brandon name him, and, of course, Brandon named him after a Dragon Ball Z character, and thus, Jiren became part of the fam.

After we got Jiren, Brandon sat me down and laid down the law. I had to stop getting animals or saying that we'd take animals without telling him, and we were done getting any more animals. Turns out two dogs, three cats, a pig, and thirty plus chickens were enough for one fellow. Who knew that that five-pound orange kitten would be the straw that broke Brandon's back. Not me! Our home became the dumping ground for friends' chickens or when people moved. Our flock went from six to forty-five in about a year. Obviously, we built a bigger fence, and the gals were all happy and healthy. Chicken Lizzo's claim to fame is being on the cover of this book, may she forever be immortalized.

What started out as a fun hobby and a way to save money on eggs (as if chicken feed isn't way more expensive than eggs are...) turned into so much more. Along the way we got goats for milk and I appreciated the still quiet mornings I'd spend milking goats, straining it, and then being able to make our own soap and cheese with it. As food prices went up our interest in being more self-sufficient did as well. A friend with a tractor tilled us up a half-acre worth of garden bed, we started swapping seeds with friends, and Brandon went back to school to study horticulture. Friends who were further along on their self-sufficient farm journey taught us about raising rabbits for meat and raising meat breed chickens. Within a year we started raising rabbits, chickens, and pigs for meat and the comfort of having full freezers full of our own organic feed fed and humanely raised and processed meat. All four boys help feed, raise, clean cages, and process our animals and help plant, weed, and harvest the garden. I'm rarely certain I am doing parenting things right, but I think in this area we are. They appreciate our animals, get excited to help Brandon cook them in new ways for supper, and each spring they fight over seed and hatchery catalogs.

Having a lot of animals is not easy. Going out of town,

daily farm chores, endless trips to the feed store. It is work. Most days it would be way easier to go to the grocery store and buy meat and eggs and vegetables. We continue to rebel against the status quo. Farming isn't for everyone, and we continue to learn daily, but knowing we grew and raised what goes in or on our bodies feels really good. We love sharing our bounties with friends and neighbors, swapping for deer meat from friends in the winter, and sharing our land with others who want to garden but don't have the space. Daily our animals bring us joy, or sustenance, and that alone makes it all worth it. Someone recently messaged me on Instagram and said that their seven-year-old asks them daily to see pictures of Meatball, so really it is all invaluable.

Part III

Fitness: Intentional Movement Each Day

11

Why I Want You to Intentionally Move Your Body and Why I'm Moving Mine

On January 1, 2018, I had an innocuous New Year's Resolution to move my body for thirty days. That was it. I had no idea that little resolution would absolutely change the trajectory of my entire life. I donned my running shoes and ran a very cold snowy run around the city block in Richmond. Looking back, I'm so annoyed I didn't take a picture of myself that day. It was nearly sunset (aka like 5 p.m. in January in Virginia), and I had been enjoying the day with Brandon but figured I had to make it day one of my resolution before quitting.

Quite a bit of time had passed since my last run, but the cold air was sharp in my lungs, and I chased the glowing orange sunset and my favorite part, I didn't have to double back because we lived in the actual city, so it was easy to run a block. After my run, I came home and declared my resolution to Brandon. He has learned to just nod and smile at all my ideas. Most are insane, but some are good, like this one! I couldn't find a proper piece of paper but grabbed a yellow memo pad I had "borrowed" from work and tore a page out and wrote <u>Workout for 30 Days</u> along the top. I numbered the pages one through thirty and put an X next to day one.

Turns out January has thirty-one days, so this was not thought out from the get-go. I didn't run every day of those thirty days, but I did discover YouTube yoga, bodyweight programs, and rock climbing at my local YMCA. Not once in the month did my brain think, "I need to lose weight, I need to be XYZ, I need to work out for this many minutes a day." Whatever the day afforded me, I did. I'd wake up early and workout before I got started with my day. No one cared about this resolution I made except myself. This was before I had an Instagram, before articles were written about me, before we had any kids. Brandon supported me and never made me feel guilty for the time I wanted to spend working out, but also never joined me. I never expected him to join me though; it was my resolution, not his! Throughout the month, I discovered ways of moving that I loved. YouTube Zumba videos were not for me, yoga was incredibly hard, and cardio remained my true love.

Besides one afternoon rock climbing pass at the local YMCA, I never spent a dollar working out that month. I didn't own any workout equipment; I borrowed the purple yoga mat from a friend (and then never returned it-sorry, Jan!)

There were a few times I'd get upset if I felt like I hadn't worked out "enough" in a day. My mindset has drastically changed since then, and even though I didn't have any specific goals in mind other than working out for thirty days, sometimes I'd still get VERY upset if I didn't feel like I did enough. A ten-minute workout is better than no workout, but it was hard for me to get to that point.

Let me tell you a little secret: I used to be very not fun when I didn't get my way. I'd like to think I've gotten better and held onto things more loosely (thank you, four kids, for making that happen), but I used to get so antsy and anxious and upset if the plan in my head didn't work out. If I'd get off work and had plans to workout but then Brandon had made plans with friends, or if the weather changed or if I needed to run unexpected errands and the plans I had made (without telling anyone) had to change, I'd get so upset. This makes me sound like a brat, and I for sure acted like one sometimes. Surprise, surprise, I used to be a control freak! I can certainly still act like that but have gotten better at communicating what is in my head to Brandon to mitigate unnecessary disappointment or stress when things don't go my way. The end of the thirty days was approaching, and I was feeling good. I felt stronger, had more energy, and was having a lot of fun trying new things, and it was nice to set aside time for myself every day to do something. I decided to keep going.

I thought, surely, if I can do this for thirty days, I can do it for fifty days. Days kept flying by, and winter worked its way out of Virginia. As the weather changed, my ability to do more outside workouts increased. I bought my first online program, a ninety-day program from a trainer named Betty Rocker, and I loved it. Betty and I hung out most every morning in my living room, watching the sunrise from our bay window doing high intensity workouts before work. I would go running with friends on the weekends, and once, I convinced Brandon to do yoga with me. Notice that I said once. I started marking off days on a white board because the days kept accruing faster than I anticipated. As fifty days approached, I treated myself to a new pair of leggings from TJ Maxx!

Day fifty came and I was still feeling good and loving my journey, so I shot for seventy-five days. You can probably guess where the story goes. I shot for one hundred and went *crazy* when I hit one hundred. One hundred straight days of working out. I had muscles! My bicep was looking like the little bicep emoji! Brandon *for sure* got tired of me walking around with my biceps flexed, pointing at things and saying welcome to the gun show. My biceps resembled a walnut a.k.a. there was nothing there but slightly more nothing than had been on January 1, and I thought I was hot stuff.

By the one-hundred-day mark, I had begun talking about this workout journey more and more. Early spring

2018, some friends who worked in the health and wellness industry asked me if I would create a five-day workout plan for them and some friends to go through. I clearly had never made a workout plan before, nor had any idea what I was doing, but by then, I had learned plenty of new body weight moves and pieced them together. Essentially, I created a workout that I would want to do every day. They were relatively quick, simple workouts that require no equipment, and I had so much fun creating them.

At this point, Feeding Tube Fitness didn't exist, and I was just sharing on social media. Occasionally, I would post what I had been learning or working on, and I shared this little five-day program I had created. Dozens of friends asked me to email it to them, and I made little videos to go along with it and emailed it to over a hundred people in a two-week period. My friends loved it and raved about it and asked me if I would create more plans for them. I spent the next four months creating a plan, writing down moves, trying out combinations of moves, and making an entire thirty-day plan. Initially, it was called "30 Days of Fitness," and it was an email subscription people could sign up for. When I tell you that literal blood, sweat, and tears went into that program, I'm not lying. I spent hours on the phone multiple times with Mail Chimp, Google, my friend Jon, and others trying to figure out how to make an automated subscription work. Every single exercise had a full exercise description, pictures, and a video of the entire workout. Along this journey, I realized how inaccessible fitness is to the disability community (more to come on that) and wanted this plan to be as accessible as possible. I figured out how to make it screen reader accessible, and by the end of it, including all thirty days, exercise descriptions, goal setting tips, motivation, and encouragement, it was over 20,000 words.

Technology finally was on my side, and the program went live online, and from the time it began till the time I pulled it offline, over 500 people went through it in a year. Fortunately for others, it was entirely free! Unfortunately for me, it was free! Eventually, I turned it into a book, which was another labor of love, shout out to Madeline who spent literal hours and tears with me trying to figure out how to make Kindle Direct Publishing work and get this baby live online. As the program evolved, so did I, and the book ended up being called *30 Days of Movement,* and it still exists on Amazon today. That wasn't a sales pitch, just one of the wild outcomes of this movement journey.

Back to working out. One hundred days became two hundred, and on day 273, I started my fitness Instagram page, @feedingtube.fitness. Mostly, I was tired of spamming my friends on other social media pages about my workouts, and a friend suggested I make a fitness Instagram. Before this suggestion, I had no idea that was even a thing that people made. On my personal account, I was posting things like sunsets, concerts, dogs I met, and just general life. I had no idea people had whole accounts dedicated to specific topics. The idea that maybe someday I could get free leggings from a brand was enough enticement to start the account, so I did. I posted a selfie while at the beach and literally never thought anyone would follow me or care. I would spend hours searching fitness hashtags, following accounts, sending messages saying hey, and still working out every day. I had no agenda other than to share daily workouts. Every post I've ever made still exists on that account, the photo and video quality are horrible, and no filters have ever been used.

Slowly, I built a little community, and people were incredibly gracious. A girl named Kayla found me and connected me with my now friend, Amy, who was the mom of a disabled son who was a personal trainer. Before meeting Amy, I didn't even know the phrase "adaptive athlete" existed. Most are familiar with the Special Olympics, and I had seen a para-athlete (another word I didn't know at the time) on the hand cycle at the Richmond Half Marathon, but other than tug-on-your-heartstrings commercials or advertisements, I had never seen disabled athletes. Instagram opened my eyes to a whole new world. As a disabled person and a disabled athlete, I'm ashamed to say that I had no idea the amount of bad-ass-ery that exists in the adaptive athlete community. Disabled men and women doing CrossFit, skiing, boxing, you name it; there are disabled people completely kicking ass. Not in an inspirational way, but in a holy crap, this girl could beat me up seven times over because of how strong she is. Again, that is inspiring, and should inspire you to move, not just say oh wow, with a single tear running down your cheek in awe. Believe me, without even knowing most of these athletes by name, I know they don't want your pity.

I also realized how incredibly able-bodied, white, thin, and typically blonde the fitness industry is. I had no idea this was what the fitness industry was like until I started my deep dive on Instagram. When I started my resolution, I didn't buy anything, I had leggings and shirts from college, but I didn't frequent athletic stores, so I wasn't very familiar with the athletic model aesthetic. Starting my Instagram account wildly opened my eyes to the reality of what the fitness world was and, starkly, what it was not, inclusive. Other companies, like Target, Tommy Hilfiger, and Aerie have gotten more inclusive and representative, but the fitness industry is seriously lacking. When people asked me why I started my Instagram, I say, "To start an inclusive fitness revolution!" I don't think I've achieved that yet, but I have partnered with several fitness clothing brands on Instagram and have modeled for them to show their customers that they are inclusive with their clothes. I've been able to partner with lots of fun and innovative fitness equipment companies. I've even partnered with Degree, the deodorant company, in their quest for an overhaul of the fitness industry. We have a *long* way to go in terms of representation, but I ain't quitting anytime soon. I have met incredible people who are on a quest for the same, and we are nothing if not a tenacious bunch!

On my quest to overhaul the fitness industry, I used every day to discover new styles of working out, new programs, new equipment, and a whole world of disabled and non-disabled athletes that I had no idea existed. It honestly felt like I was drinking from a fire hose with my eyes opened to such an amazing world. I was still trucking along, doing my thing, and working out every day and feeling good. I had been on Instagram before but had barely any followers and was not on it that often. As my fitness account grew, so did my screen time, and my envy. I would see girls who were so thin, girls doing handstands, girls doing pushups, girls who could spend hours in the gym every day, girls who were stronger, faster, and had better leggings than me. Remember when I set out on this journey and had no goals? I still didn't, but it appeared everyone else did, and they somehow seemed better off. I would get jealous of six pack abs, perfect push-up forms, and home gyms with lots of equipment I didn't have.

For a while, I became obsessed with posting on Instagram, growing my account, and doing things "right." My followers were growing because I read all the blogs about how to grow your account, how to use hashtags and analytics, and it was working. I wouldn't post and ghost, I'd interact with accounts from hashtags I liked, I would respond to every single comment, every single DM, I'd post when I was "supposed to." Typing all that out seems so silly. I have no idea why I did those things.

I was still moving every day. 365 days soon approached, and I was buying myself all the treats and planning on celebrating with my pals on Instagram. Brandon still wasn't moving with me, and honestly, most of my real-life family and friends didn't follow my fitness account. Frequently, I'd get messages that I was inspiring people to move, and I felt frustrated that I couldn't inspire my real-life people to move. Some days I'd feel resentful and annoyed that I was writing this whole book on working out, my body was looking *banging,* and this incredible tribe of people all over the globe started pouring into my little corner of the internet, but it seemed like I wasn't actually doing anything at home. Each week, I would do a post called, "Truthful Thursdays" and share real-life things. Things about my feeding tube, having a medical condition, ugly truths about myself, or just whatever I was thinking about or going through those days. Brandon doesn't even have Instagram, so I felt like I was pouring my heart out by writing online, and he never even knew. There were lots of hard lessons in those early days about communication and learning how to not be controlling. Then learning it again and again and again seemingly every day.

When I started moving, it was for me, not for anyone else. More than once along the way, I had forgotten that. Even now, four years later, I can sometimes feel beholden to these constructs I've made for myself, not for anyone else. I can still get antsy when I feel I haven't moved enough that day, but one simple shift has alleviated much of that anxiety within me.

I don't know if you noticed, but as this chapter has unfolded, I switched from saying worked out to move. Somewhere during the first year of my resolution, I stopped saying I was working out. In my head, I told myself I was intentionally moving my body every day. This simple phrase and switch in my head changed everything. Anything can be intentional movement. Walking with your kids, chasing chickens, parking far away at Walmart, spending a rainy Friday night walking around Target, crying on your bathroom floor, praying, or meditating in stillness, or laying on the floor after a feeding tube change. You may be reading this and be like uh no, those are just things anyone and everyone does when they need to; grocery shopping is not movement. Oh, but my friend, it is. Or, at least, it can be. This is much more of a mindset shift than an actual lifestyle switch.

I was still running, doing YouTube workouts, trying new things like an aerial silk class, hiking with friends, or who knows what else, but my heart and mind shifted. Instead of feeling pressured to work out every day, which in most of our minds means sweating, heart rate up, high paced, painful movements, chasing after muscle gains, etc., I set out to intentionally move every day. Anything can be intentional when you choose for it to be. I hated the thought that I was promoting and encouraging others to do something that maybe wasn't attainable to them. Friends with mobility aids weren't going to work out in the same way that I was, and if I was preaching disability inclusive activities, I wasn't going to be like, oh sorry you can't do a burpee, you can't intentionally move your body—no.

Movement looks different for everyone every day. It looks really different for me every day, especially with the addition of four kids, a farm, multiple side businesses, and life. My movement may not look like yours, today, or ever, but we can still move. My friend is in a power chair, and she and her husband take their dog for a walk together daily, and you ain't gonna ever tell me that being outside, getting some vitamin D, chatting, and being intentional about their time together around their neighborhood is not intentional movement. Sometimes my intentional movement really is sitting on my porch or in my car and crying and processing things. Sometimes I'm literally unable to physically move my body until I can process through emotions or situations or cry out to God for help, and I think moving your heart, mind, and soul are just as important as moving your body.

Releasing myself from the expectation of sweating, freed up so much more time and joy in my life. I sincerely hope that you can find ways to move your body, heart, soul, mind, whatever, every day. I'm not sure of many things in life, but I do know that this will have a positive impact on you.

Speaking of being set free, you know what else sets me free? Taking off my dang fitness tracker. I had a Fitbit for years and then an Apple watch. I know people are crazy about closing their Apple watch rings, but I am confident that if there aren't already studies about the psychology behind the rings, there will be soon. Movement should be joyful. It should be enjoyable, fun, and pressure free. Being chained to an Apple watch and being fearful of breaking your streak of closing your rings is not going to serve you. Yes, it's good accountability, but also really stressful. Just today I thought about how I liked having my Fitbit telling me to get up and move every hour and not be a work from home slug, but I can also just be an adult and set a timer on my phone or laptop or look at the dang clock and move without something on my body telling me to. You do you; I'm not out here on a crusade to burn fitness trackers, but if you've ever been stressed out because you didn't close your rings and you're staying up late getting on your stationary bike at 10 p.m. to close your ring before bed, feeling frantic about it, then it isn't serving you well!

I want to inspire you to move your body because you love it, not because you feel beholden to technology or leaderboards. In the same way that I pray and thank God before every run I have, I thank her every time I can move my body, as well as every morning when I wake up. Our bodies are freaking miracles. You may hate your body, hate the size, shape, how it feels in the world, how clothes look on it, or a million other things. But I wish you wouldn't, because your time can be used in so many better ways, and the world needs your time, energy, and dreams. If you're reading this, you have a 100 percent chance of survival, so give yourself and your body a little credit.

Moving my body every day for four years has had awesome benefits. My mental health is so much better and continues to stay healthy and good when I move, especially earlier in the day. I feel stronger than I've ever felt. My bloodwork is off the charts good (for the first time ever), and I am gaining weight for the first time ever. I'm proud of myself for sticking with something for over four years. I've met the coolest friends online and in real-life because of all this, and I'm so grateful.

12

The Time I Fell Down a Manhole, and Other Fitness Disasters

My intentional moving has not always graceful. In the fall of 2010, I fell down a manhole. Let me set the scene for you: It was early September in North Carolina, which means it was still probably hotter than the sun outside. I was a junior at a small liberal arts college. I was playing ultimate Frisbee (not to be confused with Frisbee Golf) on what was affectionately known as the quad. Most colleges have quads, I believe, but they are usually large open fields. This was a large open hill in the middle of my small campus. I also use the term "campus" loosely because, really, it was just a circle of buildings, and almost everything you would need access to was in that circle.

I was playing as I did every day at 4 p.m. I would schedule my classes to ensure that I had every afternoon open. Surely, I could have used that one-two-hour block of time every day before dinner to do homework or study, but instead, I ran up and down this hill trying to catch and throw a frisbee to my teammates. Occasionally I got hurt; I broke several toes, one or two ribs and got a black eye on that hill. There were no formal teams; whoever showed up that day showed up. Captains would be chosen, and we would size up new people. It was definitely male dominated, but there were several very badass women that would show up regularly and surely would run literal circles around the boys (here's to you, Chelsea Turlington (now Ellwood)). Sometimes people would let their competitive nature come out and take out their daily frustrations at classes, roommates, and life events, but, mostly, it was very lighthearted. Scores didn't carry over to the next day. When the games would end, we'd all high-five, and chances are most of us would walk up the hill to the cafeteria and eat dinner together. We all had different majors, different interests, different friend groups, but could easily be united on the quad.

My memories of this particular day (re: the day I fell into the manhole) are a little fuzzy, so I enacted the help of my pal Lauren to help remember the day. This next portion is mostly her words.

We were guarding each other, and I was standing behind you, but I was looking towards the Stroup dorm (the bottom of the hill) because that's where the Frisbee was. And then I heard this awful scraping sound. I just remember the metal. I don't know if you yelled, but I assume you did because then someone yelled, "Hannah?" Then half of you was in a manhole. Matt Walters asked if you saw any zombies down there.

I do remember that the Frisbee was at the bottom of the hill. I was running pretty fast to get down there to help my team out. Lauren was probably chasing me (good thing she wasn't too close behind me, or this could have been more disastrous). I remember stepping on the manhole cover in the middle of the quad. I guess they had been doing some work on it earlier that day and didn't set the cover back on it correctly. Yes, there *was* a cover on it, but it wasn't lying flat on top. Everyone always asks me how I fell into an open hole. Listen, there was a lid! It was slightly ajar but not conceivable to the naked eye, or at least someone running as fast as they could down a hill after a piece of plastic and not thinking the manhole cover wasn't on properly. The gap was not noticeable, especially in the grass on the quad.

So, I was running, full speed, down a hill, and stepped on the lid, and so the lid went *up*, and I fell *IN*. Luckily, I caught myself by my armpits and didn't fall all the way down to my death. Have you ever seen the inside of a manhole? There are metal rungs all the way down. Had little Hannah fallen all the way in, I surely would have gotten pretty banged up on those metal rungs and whatever zombies or Ninja Turtles were waiting for me at the bottom. I remember someone else higher up on the hill saying, "I literally saw you running, and then you disappeared." I pulled myself out, or maybe someone helped me out. My legs were *very* bruised and scraped up and bleeding. Naturally, I kept playing. Everyone was pretty shaken up, the boys ensured the cover was properly put back on the manhole, and everyone avoided that entire side of the field the rest of the game. I don't remember how the game ended, but since I'm the one that fell down a manhole, I'm going to tell you that my team won.

By the end of the game, my legs were already turning black and blue and still bleeding. I hobbled across the quad back to my dorm and found my best friend Chelsea. I distinctly remember saying to her "Chelsea, can you help me? I fell down a manhole and need you to help me clean my legs up." (It was mostly on the backs of my thighs.) Her response, honest to God, was, "Yeah and I just punched a shark." I was very confused at why she was talking nonsense to me, and I said, "No you didn't. I really fell down a manhole; please help me." I think at this point she still didn't believe me, and so I turned around and showed her my bruised bleeding legs, and I think she exclaimed, "Oh my God; you fell down a manhole!" She then proceeded to lay me down across all the bathroom sinks and pour alcohol and peroxide over my wounds and cleaned me up from whatever diseases were surely inside the manhole. I am fairly certain I cussed her out this entire time because of how bad it burned. She was very kind and partially sympathetic to my cause but also was very stern in telling me to be quiet because she was helping me out. What a pal!

Later that afternoon I told my friend Brittany what had happened. Brittany was always a little social justice warrior and proceeded to tell me that we were *immediately* going to campus police to tell them what had happened. I think she also told me I should sue the school, but she is also known for being a little dramatic about things. Brittany marched me to the University Police station, where, unbeknownst to me, my future best pal, Mary, was working. Mary was a freshman at the time, and this was only a week or two into school, so surely, she was a bit nervous and timid. Then, Brittany and I, who were really not at all known for being quiet or subtle women (especially when together), stormed into the police station and told Mary that I had just fallen down a manhole. This surely was not something that she had been trained to handle in her receptionist job, so I think she was a little speechless. We regaled her with the tale of my injuries and maybe filed a complaint, though I'm not sure. I think this is Mary's first memory of me, which is very hilarious.

I could barely walk the next few days and had bruises and scabs for weeks. Several weeks, or maybe months, later, someone came to actually fix the manhole. The immediate fix was to put cones around it so no one else would fall down it. The day I saw a bulldozer parked on the quad near the manhole, I left a note on the bulldozer steering wheel. I said "Thanks for fixing this manhole. Love, the girl that fell down it."

That's my tale of how I fell down a manhole. Hopefully, like all good tales, you regard this as a cautionary tale and *never* step on a manhole cover because it just may not be secured.

13
Running Stories: That's Right, Running!

Running has helped me through some rough times. I don't know if you've ever experienced your early twenties as a female (maybe males experience the same but . . . no idea), but it's not really a fun time. My friends and I would refer to this time as the shitty years (sorry, Mom). You graduate college and feel like you're an adult, but then you aren't qualified to do much of anything. So, you get a random job just because you need a job, and you have no money. You probably live with like two to five people that you may or may not like. You also feel pressure to find your soulmate. You have things you're interested in doing, but have no money, and it just all feels hard. You may cry a lot (I did). You're not yet established as a person, and you're shedding your previous high school and college and young adult identities and coming into your own, but you may not really know who that is. It's so hard.

If you're in your early twenties, my hats off to you. It is a hard and sad and weird time. No one really prepares you for it either. I'll say this though—it gets so much better. I'm of the mindset that it's all uphill from here. I'm only thirty-one, but it's so good. So much better than twenty-one. I have no desire to ever go backwards in my life. I thought I was confident and strong and self-assured years ago, but now I know that it is so much better than I could have ever imagined. All the time, I tell Brandon I can't wait to be forty, and he does not feel the same. He had a little existential crisis when he turned thirty. Finding gray hairs on my head brings me so much joy.

I *am* a runner, but it is not at all my sole identity, nor do I even run weekly now, but for a while in my life, I did. It's actually a hard balance with having a feeding tube. I love running. I love high intensity workouts. I love cardio. It's not because I'm trying to lose weight or look a certain size. If anything, I'm trying to gain weight. It's a hard balance between loving cardio but then having to work really hard to supplement those calories I lost. In my movement journey, I've found other things I love too, but running is the best, free therapy I've ever experienced. Most of this book was born on walks and runs when I'd left my phone at home and had ideas or remembered stories that are funny and should be shared. But, ask me to run on a treadmill, and I'd rather do literally anything else. It's outside or nothing for me. Running helped me find myself.

The next two stories involve running, but no lasting injuries or permanent fears.

In college, a few friends were planning on running a half marathon. The only running I ever did was playing frisbee every day, so in reality, I probably hadn't ever run more than like a mile intentionally. But I'm not one to miss out on fun, so I boldly exclaimed that I was going to join them and run a half marathon too! We decided this early in the fall, and the half marathon was in December (which is a really dumb time to run a half marathon and train for one). I remember telling my parents, and my dad laughing at me and telling me there was no way I could run a half marathon. *Boom.* Signed up that night, paid my registration fee, made a training schedule, and did the dang thing. I don't know why the people in my life haven't harnessed this power more often—to get me to do something, all that needs to happen is to tell me I can't do it. It wasn't so much that my dad didn't have faith in my ability . . . it was more so the fact that I had never run more than a mile and that I have a trach that I breathe through, and typically people with trachs aren't out here running many miles.

I was committed. I paid the painfully high registration fee for a college student and had charts and schedules for runs posted all over my dorm room. Have I mentioned that I lived in a one stoplight town aka . . . doing long distance runs essentially meant you were running in a circle around the town or running in a straight line out of town then just turning back around. There is nothing I hate more than having to run out to a halfway point and turn around.

Looking at the same scenery for X number of miles is *painfully* boring to me. At the time, I did not listen to music, podcasts didn't exist, or at least were not popular with college kids (Why is this such a depressing sentence?), and audiobooks were not my jam. To be honest, I had that phone that looked like a little Nokia on the outside but flipped open and had a keyboard on the inside. That thing was handy and shaped like a brick, but alas, no music was pumping through the tiny speaker. Running out and back was the worst, but running in circles around the same town was also the worst. Plus, one part of campus has a giant hill affectionately called the widow-maker because that dude will kill you, especially if you have to run it multiple times in a one run period.

Naturally part of my training routine involved a rest day, which is when I'd play ultimate frisbee. Our little training team had a doctor/track coach on it, and he was very not happy when he found out I wasn't actually resting. I was just running up and down the quad on my off days. Don't tell him that I played frisbee on my regularly scheduled running days too. I loved frisbee. What could I say? I'd have one day a week where I was supposed to do cross training, which was supposed to be lifting weights, so I'd go to our college gym and bop around lifting like five-pound dumbbells and acting like my arms were very strong and powerful (they were not . . . I was basically just a hot dog torso with noodles for appendages).

I was faithful to my schedule though. I'd run every time I was supposed to run, even if I didn't feel good, even if I should have been studying, even if it was raining out. My stubborn will to prove my dad wrong was a very good driving factor. Honestly, running a half marathon is attainable to most able-bodied people. It is hard and stretches you and takes a lot of training, but it is not impossible (as you'll find out in another story). Nearing the end of my training as the half marathon date was quickly approaching, I started to get extremely bored of running in this little town. I'm not going to pretend like I didn't complain about it, oh . . . constantly . . . to my friends, aka my best friend and roommate Chelsea. One Sunday I had to do my longest long run yet, ten miles. I had been psyching myself up for it and knew I could physically do it, but the thought of having to run *ten miles* in this town made me so reluctant to do it. I spent hours leading up to the day of the run looking on google maps and mapping my run, trying to figure out how I could make a new and exciting route appear out of nowhere.

I guess all my complaining got to Chelsea because after church and lunch, as I was tying up my laces, still hoping a magical new road would appear out of nowhere, Chelsea (who was an athlete and runner) told me to get in her car and she'd take me to a new route. I was game and entirely too trusting, so I packed my sports bra full of gauze for my feeding tube (she was leaky) and hopped in her jeep. We drove and talked and laughed, and I wasn't really thinking about where we were going. We drove past the river, which was 3.2 miles from campus, and kept going. I was enjoying my time with her and not really thinking about what we were doing or where we were going. We kept driving, kept driving, and eventually passed the, "Welcome to South Carolina" border sign. Okay . . . okay . . . this was becoming less fun of a drive, but we kept going. Suddenly, Chelsea pulled over on the side of the road and told me to get out. Literally the side of the road, no parking lots or sidewalks were involved. I politely asked her if she had lost her mind, and she said that we were ten miles from campus and that I better get to running. Did I mention she is my *former* best friend? Just kidding.

So, I literally got out of her car, and she did a U-turn and left me in the dust. While standing on the side of the road thinking that my best friend had dropped me off in another state ten miles away from where I lived, I realized that I didn't have to double back! I could run in a straight line for 10 miles along country, rolling hills! No circles were involved, no running out and back. Hooray! Chelsea was a genius! Good thing it was a straight line since I didn't have a GPS or anything; I actually don't even think I had a cell phone. I just had my little chicken legs and an open road. So, I started running.

Every time I start a run, even now, miles and years and states later, I tell God thank you. Thank you for letting me lace up my shoes, thank you for fresh air, thank you for open roads to run on, and thank you for a body that is able to run. I do all this before I even take a single step. I never know how my runs will be. Will I get cramps early on? Will my stomach decide it hates me and leak out everything that has ever been inside me? Will I be able to finish what

I set out to do? Who knows? But I thank God anyway even without all the answers because having access to free, open air without much fear of things in my surrounding areas is really nice. If I were to run a country ten miles now, I'd for sure have a phone and people other than Chelsea to know where I was, but I'd still be really grateful for open roads. I ran and ran and ran. I secretly love country roads because I would take hills over flat, boring land that stretches for miles and miles any day. Give me variety and challenges and reliefs.

I was just running along thinking about whatever a twenty-year-old has to think about, and suddenly, I was running along a fence with a lot of cows in it. I was saying "Hi" to every cow I passed, and then I looked over and *the cows were running too*! At first, I thought, *"Oh my gosh; I am in the Lion King!"* And I started singing songs from the soundtrack, but then I realized that at some point their fence has to end, and suddenly I could be in a stampede situation, and that seemed much less fun. So, I ran along and prayed that they knew how and when to stop ahead of their fence and that I didn't somehow incite an entire field of cows to be set loose in South Carolina. When I say the cows were running too, I'm not talking like one or two . . . I'm talking dozens. I guess they were bored too, saw me running, and thought, "Well, I have nothing to do today except chew this cud, so why not have a little frolic along?"

I could see the end of the fence ahead of me, and luckily the cows did start to slow down. Cows apparently are smart enough to know about fences and to not mess with them, because not a single one tried to come through the fence at the end and get me. Whew. That was enough adrenaline to get me through the rest of the ten miles and back to my dorm. Chelsea loves this story and considers herself the author of me getting to run with the cows (I don't think they were bulls but that would be a cooler story).

*　*　*

Another time, still in my early twenties, I was in grad school getting my master's degree in social work, living with my brother and sister-in-law, working at least three jobs, and going to school full-time. I was a bouncer at a concert venue, worked at Gap/Old Navy, and did some pet sitting and other hella random things at once. There was nothing outwardly bad about my life; I was in a great small group of girls at the church I went to, had other friends, loved grad school, and loved living closer to my family after I had been living in Brazil the past year, but dang if something wasn't missing. Turns out nothing was missing; I was just young and dumb and thought I was grown when I wasn't.

Richmond has a huge half marathon and marathon every November. It's one of the friendliest marathons and super popular, and the entire city shuts down. I had run several half marathons before this one, but those all involved training. On a whim the week before the half marathon, I decided I was going to run it. No training had occurred. No thought really had occurred. I just decided I was going to ghost run it, which is not good, and you shouldn't do it. I didn't have enough money to sign up and tried to find friends who had backed out and would sell me their bibs, but no such luck. I read blogs on ghost running and figured out the best way to do it. I literally just decided, "Oh I can do that!" So, I used photoshop and *made a fake bib*. Y'all, I am for sure going to hell for this. Friends were posting their bibs on Facebook the night before, and I literally made a fake one and printed it out and tried to guess the size. Somehow, I convinced my brother to drop me off the next morning with my fake bib safety pinned to my shirt. It was November, so it was cold out, and I had lots of layers on so when we lined up at the starting line, I very quickly pulled up my top layers and flashed the race guy my bib and quickly covered it back up. My brother told me to text him if I needed to be picked up early and we'd figure out how to make that happen even though the entire city was shut down.

My friend Christine lived about four miles into the thirteen miles, so I figured if nothing else, I'd just go camp out at her house till it ended. I put myself in one of the last waves of runners because, hello, I had no training. My entire training consisted of running sprints up and down the hill I lived on for five minutes one afternoon. Even that exhausted me, so I'm not sure why I thought I could run 13.1 miles without training, but again, I was young and dumb. Part of the shitty years is that you do somehow feel invincible. That's wrong. But you feel that way, so you do things like run races you aren't ready for. The most extensive part of my training was the time I spent buying Amy Poehler's book, *Yes Please!* I had never bought an audiobook before; it seemed like a good idea to try the same day I tried running a race I wasn't ready for.

My brother dropped me off, and the gun went off, and I started running. To say I was freezing is an understatement. It was *so* cold and rainy, and I instantly regretted everything. I decided not to listen to anything for the first few miles to get myself settled in. I needed something to look forward to. Everything was pretty okay, minus the cold at first. Regardless of how far I run, I always think the first three miles are the hardest. This is unfortunate if you're only running three miles because it doesn't ever get easy, but if you're running more than three, it does get better. The first three went by fairly quickly, and I hadn't stopped to walk at all. When I set out running, I told myself my only goal was to finish. I could walk, take breaks, do whatever I needed to. I had times in my head from my prior marathons (my best was 2:22), but I was okay with whatever; I just wanted to prove to myself that I could do it. See, again, young and dumb.

Races that you pay for (ahem, most of them) include snacks and beverages along the route. Before setting off, I vowed to myself I would not take anything that was offered to me. I had a little water bottle with me, but I was not going to use resources I didn't pay for. See, I'm not a total monster! Anytime there was a time check thing (You know the things on the ground you run over with your little time chip in them that sends an update to the leaderboards), I would literally dive off the track into the bushes or something to avoid running over it. This probably wasn't necessary in hindsight since I didn't have a timer chip in my photoshopped bib, but I didn't want to mess up the leaderboards *or* get caught in my ghost running scheme.

Around mile five, I was freezing and hating everything. I hadn't warmed up at all, and it was miserable. I pulled my phone out to text my brother, and my fingers were literally too cold to text. I tried multiple times and couldn't even open the messages app, so I figured it was a sign from above to keep going. At mile six, I started Amy's book, and we were running through a park. A para-athlete was ahead of me on a racing wheelchair hand bike and was crushing a giant uphill. A band was playing, and the crowd was cheering him on; Amy was really funny, and I finally felt like I could do this and not die. I was running and legitimately laughing out loud, feeling really good. Who knew it would only take six, freaking miles? I honestly wasn't feeling tired at this point, still feeling good and hadn't had to walk much. The course runs through parks and neighborhoods and downtown and all over the city, so there were always new things to look at, and it never double backed on itself. Praise the Lord.

Amy carried me through till about mile nine, then I was back to regretting every decision I had ever made that had gotten me to this point. I got to mile ten, and they were handing out shots of whiskey, and I knew I had vowed to not take anything that didn't belong to me, but I just needed it! I snagged a shot and threw it back and swallowed like I had never swallowed before. The last three miles were filled with spectators cheering us all on and yelling that we were almost there! The whiskey got me through the last three miles, and I flew. The finish line was finally in sight, and I couldn't believe that I was so close. Unfortunately, there were literally barricades on either side of the finish line, so I couldn't avoid the time chip. I felt really bad running across it without a time chip and prayed that I wouldn't be messing anything up for any other runner participating. Oops, sorry! I made it across the finish line in two hours and thirty-two minutes, only ten minutes slower than the races I had *trained for.*

I crossed the finish line elated, there were people cheering for me, and a man tried to hand me a medal and a warm blanket. Instead of taking them or even speaking to him like a normal person, I just kept running. He probably thought I was crazy. I violently shook my head no at him as I ran past him. Here's the thing. The race ends at the bottom of a hill but to get anywhere that cars would be, you must walk up a giant hill. Like half a mile at least up a straight incline. My brother was waiting at the top of the hill, which is the closest he could get with all the road closures. I swear that was the worst part of the entire day, walking up that dang hill. I probably couldn't walk up it without my calves cramping on a normal day, but after running thirteen miles, it was sheer pain. At one point, I started walking up backwards in hopes that somehow that would hurt my calves less. It didn't.

We made it home, and then I laid in bed drinking a Lime-A-Rita and watching Gilmore Girls, sure that I'd never walk again. Except, the next day, I had to go to work at Gap. I literally hobbled in with my legs looking like a sumo wrestler, wincing with every step, with my coworkers *very* bewildered as to why I looked like I had just been riding a horse all day. It took me ages to bend over to pick up off the ground T-shirts and jeans that rude customers had knocked over that I had to refold. Every single step was agony.

The good news is the pain only got worse! If you are any kind of athlete, you know that day two is worse than day one after whatever event you put your body through, and then day three is somehow even worse. The same is true for surgery recovery too though. Maybe everything in life is worse on day three. On day three, I went to my internship and had a meeting with my supervisor, Claire. I knew Claire had been training hard for the half marathon, and I was so excited to hear about her experience. She recounted her journey, and I told her mine. She was super pissed at me because I had a faster time than she did without training. My bad, Claire!

What is the morale of all this? Who knows. Do hard things. Play hard with your friends. Move your body however feels good. Do things that challenge and scare you, because you can for sure do things that you think you can't, and then they make fun stories to share forever!

Part IV
The Moon is Round and Other Moments of Advocacy and Motivation

14

The Moon is Round

Have you ever heard a story that changed your life? Chances are the story I'm about to tell you will change your life. As for the rest of the book, I'm not sure, but here's to hoping. I'll tell you right now; I'm not a night person. I hate staying up late. I don't wish to indulge in late-night talks about life. The fact that I heard this story was born out of a serious case of FOMO (Fear of Missing Out) when I was a young college gal. I'm over thirty and will routinely kick people out of my house—at like 9 p.m., even if we are having a party. Sit on the porch with me and talk for hours while the sun is up—sure thing. Cry while we are driving in the daylight hours? I'm your girl. Try to get me to be productive or deep after 8 p.m., and I'll probably fight you.

One night I was in a crowded room of college-aged kids in the mountains of North Carolina. I worked at a summer camp for high school kids. I was a baker in the kitchen and would wake up early every day to make rolls, loaves of bread, cinnamon rolls, and entirely too many cookies. Being a baker was perfect for me since we've already established that I hate staying up late. Wake me up early, let me off work early afternoon, and I am living my best life. At night, while the camp program staff (aka the real adults) were running camp, we would get to hang out in the staff cabins. Games were usually played, boys would bring out their guitars to make all the girls swoon, and many deep conversations were had on those scratchy couches. Wagon Wheel being played for the third time every night was usually my signal to head to bed, but one night I decided I would stay up late. The cutest boy I had ever seen was playing guitar, and I was clearly swooning. He was from Nashville, and I was *certain* that he would *swoon* after me too, and I would move to Nashville, and he'd get a record deal, and the rest of my life would be great. I promise you I was wearing teal Crocs, and there is a 100 percent chance he was *not* swooning over me (insert single tear emoji here). Slowly as more and more people went to bed and the crowded game room thinned out, stories began to flow. The cute boy put his guitar down and started telling stories from Nashville. Being that I was in college in a small, one-stoplight town in North Carolina, everything he said seemed exciting and enchanting. Story after story flowed, but one caught my ear. I didn't know at the time that it would change my life or become tattooed on my left bicep years later, but here we are. This is not my story, nor was it the cute boy's story, but I hope to do the story justice.

The stars aligned, and the moon was round that night. I heard a story that has transformed every day of my life since, no exaggeration needed.

Once there was a girl who had terminal cancer. She had journals and journals filled with the phrase, "The Moon is Round." After she passed away, her family was trying to figure out what this phrase meant, and finally, at the end of one of her journals, she had written that this phrase was how she saw life. The moon is always round, even if we don't always see the entire moon. We can go outside and see just a sliver, a half-moon, or a new moon. Regardless of what we physically see, the moon is always round. The shape never changes. Reflections and what we see may change, but the moon remains the same. This analogy applies to everything in life as well. There is always more to the story than we can see and know. As the story goes, she was a believer in Jesus and God, and this is how she perceived God as well. God was always present, always there, and there was always more at play than she could see. Oftentimes we get glimpses of the whole picture or see or feel God in a complete way, but that's rare—like one day a month rare—sometimes not even once a month. We continue to have hope that the full moon will shine again, but we can't make it show up any faster. We just wait. The moonlight is simply a reflection of the sun, which is still much bigger and brighter than the moon itself. The moon remains round, regardless of what reflection of it we can see.

I have googled this story countless times over the years to find the original author. I don't know if the cute boy even knew the girl or if he had just heard it anecdotally, but I'm so glad I heard it. The simple fact that I was in the room, I stayed up late, and the cute boy decided to share it was divinely timed, and I am forever grateful.

I could stop writing this book now because that's all you need to know about how I approach life. *The moon is always round.* Your story is always going to be complete; there is always a light at the end of the tunnel, things are constantly shifting and changing, and there is more brightness than we can see. This phrase has gotten me through, honestly, everything since then. I have taken hundreds of pictures of the moon because of it. (Side note: I recently saw a funny meme about how rude it is that pictures of the moon always come out awful, and I could not agree with that sentiment more.) It is rude and unfortunate because the moon is the freaking best. In my early 20s, I decided that I had to have a moon tattoo. This would not be my first tattoo and not my last, but I knew that the story and phrase would stick with me forever, and I needed a constant reminder. Turns out I'm *not* an artist, so a friend's little sister drew me a half-moon and wrote, *the moon is round* on top of the half-moon to make it round. The tattoo is on my left bicep, and it has grown as my muscles have grown, and many tattoos later, it remains my favorite. When people see the tattoo, they laugh, "Haha yeah, the moon is round, of course, duh, it's a sphere." Depending on how much I like them or not, I'll tell them the real story behind it.

My phone can predict the phrase; all I need is to type *the moon,* and it fills in the rest. Not one day in my thousands of days on earth has the moon not been round. There has always been more to my story than I have known, even though that's a lot of days to live. There is still more. Scientists say that the moon only reflects 3-12 percent of the sun's brightness. That is up to 97 percent that we don't even see. That's so much, y'all!

When things feel crappy, when I've gotten my heart broken, when I haven't gotten jobs, when adoptions have taken forever, when my minivan breaks down, when I fall down a manhole, when Brandon didn't propose when I thought he would, the moon is and was always round. There was always more that I didn't know. For instance, I didn't *know* Brandon was going to propose to me in our very tiny kitchen with all our friends since he had led me to believe it was going to happen the day before at the top of city hall overlooking the city, but this way was better. There's always more to the story (I guess, even if that story sometimes involves your future husband deceiving you for the greater good . . . maybe). That's a trite example, but it applies to *everything.* Not a day goes by that I don't say the phrase. It has become a staple mantra in our house. Someone spills milk; oh well, *the moon is round*. When we lose out on what we *thought* was our dream house—*the moon is round*. When I've had scary pap smear results—*the moon is round* (said really angrily!). I've cried those words, screamed those words, begged those words, thrown rocks saying those words, prayed those words, and whispered them over and over in the darkest of times.

The phrase itself has sustained me, but the story behind it fortifies me. I believe in and follow Jesus, and knowing that there is *always* more, there *has* to always be more. I'm not here to be naïve and assume that the *more* there is to a story is always better; it's not always better. There's no toxic positivity here, but in my experiences, knowing there is often more to the story is always better than not knowing more. When you don't get a job you hoped for, having the knowledge of why, what you could do better in an interview, or continuing to hone your skills will always benefit you in the long run, even if not getting that job sucks. I am certain that I'm not the only one who has broken up with someone and been completely heartbroken and felt like there was never anything better to come, only to fast forward five years and social media stalk that person to find out that no, in fact, my life would not have gotten better by staying with him. Actually, for this story, I went on social media and found the cute boy. He's still cute and did ultimately put out a record in Nashville, but he does *not* look like the kind of dude who would be okay with me bringing home ducklings and chickens on the regular, so we will keep Brandon. The hope and expectation that there must always be more are all I need most days.

As Maya Angelou said, "Now that I know better, I do better." Sometimes we do get to see the whole picture, and that's really dope too.

The moon story is my guiding light; my hope is that it will guide you along too. The moon is round right now as you are reading and will be round when you finish it too. My gratitude for you will only increase, though. As Shania Twain said, "Let's go, girls!" (and not just girls but all genders because all are welcome here!).

15

Bad Hours Don't Equal Bad Days

Several months ago, I was having a really bad day. Similar to Alexander and his "terrible, horrible, no good, very bad day." Mine was a bad day, and it was only 10 a.m. I texted a friend to complain about my perfectly horrible day and told her my kids had been misbehaving, I had computer troubles, and I was sad about a fight with Brandon the night before. She reminded me that it was only 10 a.m. and that the day could, in fact, turn around. She said I didn't have to write the entire day off yet, as there was still like ten more hours before I went to bed at 8 p.m. that night and eleven more hours if I wanted to be a party animal and stay up till 9 p.m.! I thought about this, texted her back, and told her she was right; I was having some bad hours, but it didn't have to be a bad day. *Boom.*

Thus, the nugget of, "Bad hours don't equal bad days" was born. There is no shame in admitting that the bad hours are really bad. Things were not going super well that morning, and there is no sugar coating that fact. But I didn't have to assume the next eleven hours were going to follow suit, nor did I have to choose to let them. Our outside circumstances can change at a moment's notice, but our reaction and our internal responses don't have to waiver. Much easier said than done, I know. I am sure that with four kids and a generally chaotic life, more "bad" things happened later that afternoon, but I immediately started to recognize them and just let them come. Just like a bad hour doesn't equal a bad day, a bad five minutes doesn't equal a bad hour. That isn't to say that bad days don't exist. I've had some truly bad days, and I know you have too. But a bad day doesn't equal a bad week, a bad week doesn't equal a bad month, and a bad month doesn't equal a bad year.

I am a very strong believer in naming your emotions. By giving your emotions a name, you can either give it power or take its power away. We talk with our kids incessantly about naming their feelings. They aren't super great at this, but to be honest neither am I most days. We have found time and time again that when we can get them to take the time to name their emotions, they don't struggle to process or cope as much and regulate easier. When they don't, everything is way harder than it needs to be, and everyone usually ends up in tears. Naming the hard things allows them to feel much more surmountable. We can tackle things that we know.

When everything is overwhelming and scary and we don't know where to act or turn, it's paralyzing.
I shared this concept on social media, and other than telling people to get gas at night instead of in the morning (do it), it is my most referred-to concept. I get messages daily about the concept, and I shared it well over a year ago. I get dozens of messages saying this concept must go in the book and that the concept has changed their lives. Here is just one powerful comment about this concept: "I am able to see things for what they are instead of writing things off and assuming that the rest of the hour, day, week, will be complete garbage."

Such a perspective takes a lot of intentionality. If you want to get really deep in the sauce, you can start figuring out why things are perceived as good or bad to you. Bad is typically just things that didn't suit my idea of what my afternoon should look like—probably not good or bad—just outside of my control and my idyllic picture of a Tuesday afternoon. Usually, my perception of good or bad external things just relates to how controlling I'm being in the moment. If I have a free afternoon with no plans and am just chilling, and my dog has explosive diarrhea on the kitchen floor, it's gross but probably not the end of the world if I'm just hanging out. If I was running out the door to meet a friend after work and then the dog had explosive diarrhea, whew... that'll probably put me in a spiral because that messed with my plans, my control for the day.

Please know I'm not out here spreading toxic positivity. Bad hours and bad days are real. There is no amount of sunshine and rainbows or Hallmark cards to convince anyone otherwise. A single phone call can completely alter your life and seem to shatter hopes, dreams, and plans. A year ago, I got a phone call that my jaw was broken. Not just my jaw, but the titanium plates and screws that had previously been holding my jaw together were also all broken. I cried so much when I found out and was so heartbroken and upset and felt like it was the end of the world. I had a lot of bad hours. Then more bad hours and bad days after having surgery and having screws screwed into the top and bottom of my jaw and having to have my mom and Brandon figure out how to put rubber bands on them. It was all the worst.

One of my favorite concepts in life is the concept of ebenezers. Merriam Webster dictionary says ebenezer means: a commemoration of divine assistance. Or, a stone of help. In the Bible, it says the stone that Samuel erected was a constant reminder to the nation of Israel that God had protected them and led them to victory (1 Samuel 7:12). God was their helper, in other words, and the Ebenezer was a visual reminder of that truth. I can't remember when I first learned of the concept of ebenezers, probably sometime in high school, but I've been obsessed with them ever since.

We all know how it feels to feel like nothing would ever go right again or where hope felt distant. But then, the light cracks through, the moon waxes, and then things that you've only dreamed or prayed would happen, start to happen. The tides turn. Despite all the phases and changes, the moon is always round regardless of what we see. Those are the times that are the best to mark. When hope springs up out of nowhere. Hours move along regardless of if we name them good or bad, so name them what they are and mark the good ones. Bad hours and hard seasons do all eventually end. Your people are rooting for you and here for you in the meantime.

16

If You Can Feed Six Chickens, You Can Feed Thirty-Six Chickens

The most chickens we've ever had at once is forty-five, but we started out with six. Who knows how many we have now? Some of them just free range around the yard all day every day. Once I had to chase a chicken with one eye across the road because she was going rogue! A friend was thinking about getting some backyard chickens and was asking for some advice about how many to get (this was when we had like forty-five) and I said, "It honestly doesn't matter how many you have, if you can feed six chickens, you can feed thirty-six chickens!" I was stunned by my brilliance. My friend was not.

That's a good life lesson, y'all! It really is true for chickens though—you're buying fifty-pound bags of feed at a time anyway. Tractor Supply doesn't sell smaller quantities, and it has an expiration, so if you have all that feed anyway, might as well not stop at six chickens! Unless you live in a neighborhood or city where you can only have six chickens. I'm not trying to have animal control come after me for *anything* in life, so I'm not here to advocate for more than six chickens. Although, when we lived in the suburbs, we were only allowed six and we had ten, so maybe that's not entirely true. You know I'm a rebel! Now we live in the country and can do whatever we want.

I texted this nugget of wisdom to all of my friends. Rarely do I claim to know what's going on or feel a stroke of brilliance, but I knew this was a good truth. Many now know the phrase, "We can do hard things," that Glennon Doyle Melton taught us all, which became a mantra for me the minute I heard it. Clearly, I don't want to plagiarize one of my idols, but I don't think Glennon even likes chickens, so I don't think she will get mad about equating this phrase with hers. If you can feed six chickens, you can feed thirty-six. You can do hard things. You can do things that don't seem possible to do. You can rebel against your neighborhood laws (just kidding, sort of)! Have you forgotten that we are a rebellious crew? You have more power, strength, and fortitude within you than you really know. In life, you will also be handed metaphorical big bags of chicken feed with more than you need, and you'll get to dip into those excess resources and have incredible times of growth that you didn't think were possible.

When I texted my friends my truth bomb, my friend Amanda said, "We must put that on a shirt." We are both impulsive and chase fun, so I immediately found a website where you can create mock-ups of any design on T-shirts, sweatshirts, mugs—whatever you want. Then you can sell the items directly to customers. Many people do this to raise money for a specific cause, but I did it to raise money for myself—feed for these forty-five chickens (how silly I was to think there wouldn't be a difference in feeding this larger flock!) The idea was funny and cute, and the shirts were really awesome. I shared on my social media and the orders came rolling in. I posted about it a few times, but I wasn't giving it much thought by tracking sales or posting it every day. I didn't even notice when the payment was deposited. Two years after the campaign ended, I used the same website to make a new design, and I was shocked to see that I made over $500 on those dang chicken shirts. I didn't even know! The shirts went out in the world, and I smile every time I see mine in my drawer. I'm proud of myself that I can do things like this. Never had I ever designed T-shirts before or advertised them, but it was really easy (thanks websites), and my people love me and love supporting me, and even the act of putting that all together on a whim totally embodied the principle. If I can have an idea at 8 p.m. while texting with a college friend and within two hours execute it and have the shirts be live online and ready to order . . . what can't I do?!

Sometimes I do hard things just to do hard things. I don't always think things through in the moment, but sometimes that's where the best work comes from—when we shut our brains off and just experience things. Every year on May 30, CrossFitters around the globe complete the Murph Challenge to honor Navy SEAL, LT. Michael P. Murphy, who passed away in service to our country. The Murph Challenge is a one-mile run, followed by 100 pull-ups, 200 push-ups, 300 air squats, and it ends with another one-mile run. I have actively been doing CrossFit for a while now and still can't fathom finishing this entire workout in one day. Two years ago, I decided I was going to do *some* of it—not even all of it. I did the first run, the 300 squats, 200 pushups, 100 crunches, and then attempted to do the second run but thought my legs were going to snap.

I didn't even do them all in order. I'd do fifty squats, twenty pushups, twenty crunches and start over until all my reps were done. I'm not sure if you've ever done 300 squats, but like . . . don't. For the next week, it took me a solid ten minutes to sit down low enough for my butt to hit the toilet seat and another ten minutes to come back up. In all honesty, I saw people on Instagram doing the Murph Challenge, and I thought *oh sure, let's do it,* as if I was at all prepared; I was not. I want to say, "Nothing can prepare you for this," but that's for sure not true. Doing CrossFit can prepare you. Being a Navy SEAL can for sure prepare you. Working out for thirty minutes a day, lifting light weights, and having chronic feeding tube pain does not prepare you. I did the dang thing though. Dang near took me out, but I did it.

At one point, Brandon came upstairs where I had been for well over half an hour and asked me what I was doing. When I shared the workout with him, he looked horrified and then told me to have fun. I told him if he heard my body hit the floor, he should probably come running. Luckily, I did not ever hit the floor and eventually finished the challenge, including the second mile run. Never did I think that I could do all that in one day, but I did.

Every single thing in my life is something that I never thought I could do. We tend to not give ourselves enough credit for how incredible we are, how far we've come in life, and the awesome things we can do. When I was born, doctors told my parents I'd never walk or talk. Everything since then has been a miracle. When you start looking for miracles, you see them all around you. Like that psychology concept of thinking about a blue car and then you see blue cars everywhere. If you are thinking of ways that you have done hard things before, you'll remember so many hard things that you've done!

Write them down, celebrate them, mark them with photos or trips. Every single thing has been a miracle and surprising and incredibly hard. You may not be like me and do things just to see if you can do them, but I would encourage you to do things that are out of your comfort zone. There has never been a time where I have regretted doing something hard. Never. Hard workouts, hard conversations with friends, saying yes to fostering teenagers, being convinced that I can fit trees into my Nissan Versa, or convincing Brandon that we should have four cats. It's all been beyond worth it. So often you hear of people at the end of their lives or after a scary diagnosis share a litany of things that they regret *not* doing. Rarely do you hear that they regret taking the risks, making the call, getting on the flight, or sharing how they feel. Yeah, the results may not always be what you want, but the results rarely matter. The act of doing the bold thing, getting out of your comfort zone, and moving forward even if you're scared, is where the secret sauce is.

How do you do hard things? You can be like me and not think about them and just go in blind and ignorant (it's bliss, right?). You can do the opposite of that and make an extensive pro-cons/list and think rationally about all the options you have ahead of you and weigh the outcomes. I'm not knocking logic; as someone who is logical but lets her emotional side win out more than the logical side of things often, I'm here for the logic. But I think if you do that, you'll talk yourself out of whatever the thing is. Chances are there is more in the world saying don't do the thing. When I think too much, I get paralyzed. Even today, thinking back on funny dating stories, I have some not funny ones that were reckless and dumb and could have ended horribly. I'm not proud of those things, but when I think about them, they were instant gratification sorts of decisions during the shitty years, not things that required work and effort and consideration. I'd venture to say that the easy things, the things that we think we can do to skate by or to hit the dopamine, are the things that can ultimately be the most reckless and damaging. This is why people give up on their dreams and hard things.

Brandon and I have a vision and a hope to bring an accessible playground and community garden to our little town. There is a big accessible playground about an hour away, but nothing close to us or the surrounding counties. This dream came to us very spontaneously, and like most things in our lives, it took hold to us, and we began the process of making it become a reality!

Dreaming the dream was very fun, but making a multi-million-dollar playground become a reality is much less fun. Believe me, *nothing* about trying to buy land and build an accessible playground and community garden in our town is easy. It's one of the hardest things I've ever tried to do. Others in our town have tried before us. They've had the same vision, caught the same wave, and have given up, and I know why. It's hard. I told someone the other day I wish I had known how hard it would be when I started, and they said no you don't, because you would have never begun. She was dang right. I wouldn't have.

If you had told me at the start of the Murph Challenge how bad my legs would hurt for the following week, I would have for sure not done it. If I had known how insanely hard parenting kids with trauma who were half my age would be, I would have run the other way. When you're in the middle of a hard thing, it's the worst. That's when you call your best friends crying on the bathroom floor telling them you can't do it anymore. You send the SOS texts. You pray for everything to just disappear (is this just me?), but you keep going.

In our case, we have kids in our home who need us to continue parenting them, despite how often they may indicate to us that they'd rather not have us parent them. Food still has to be put on the table. Showers still need to be taken. You can only sit on the bathroom floor for so long. Something else to remember: the hard things end. Hard seasons end. You are capable of enduring things. Even if the thing doesn't work out how you think it'll work out, it'll still end. Whether the ending is feeling embarrassed as you did the thing, the break room chatter about your bold move, or your inability to walk upright without being in pain—it all ends.

Yes, I know things in life are permanent, like death, but we ain't talking about death, okay. We are not often taught how to trust ourselves. You know yourself better than anyone. You know yourself better than a pro/con list of possible outcomes others have faced in your situation. If a hard thing is calling your name, or if it just pops up one day and you decide to act upon it, trust yourself!

In grad school, I wouldn't tell a single soul about a dude I was dating (besides always sending my friend Jan my location because, safety first) because I wanted to figure things out without others' opinions. Rarely did any dude last past the third date, so I saved myself and my pals a *lot* of undue listening to dumb boy drama. If I had told Brandon ahead of doing the Murph Challenge, he would have for sure told me that was insanity, and I should not spend a Saturday like that. He's fairly convincing, so I probably would have listened to him and not tried it. I didn't know I could do it, but I knew I could try, and I didn't want to be talked out of trying. Obviously, this doesn't apply to everything. If you are going through hard things, don't do them alone. I'm convinced that nearly everything in life is more fun with your people. I'm just saying at the onset of a hard thing, it's okay to make the decision to do the hard thing alone, then tell people as you go along. Your people want to help you. Your people want to join you. Whether you have lots of friends in your immediate vicinity or exclusively pals online, they are rooting for you. Way more people in life want to see you succeed than fail. So, prove the ones cheering you on right, and prove the ones doubting you wrong, and do the hard thing!

Listen, if you're like, "Hey, I don't care to do hard things," awesome! None of this is peer pressure to do hard things to brag about them. Nah, friends, we aren't about that life. I just want to gently show you that you can do these things. You can. It's in you! This is some *Lion King* Simba/Mufasa stuff where Simba looks in the pond and thinks he sees Mufasa's reflection but really, it's his own. I'm just here to offer you hope and hold up the mirror for you to see that anything and everything is possible.

I know it seems daunting and scary and you'd really rather not disrupt everything in your life. Believe me, there have been times when I've looked at Brandon and been like, "Why did we give up our fun, young, married lives where we could go anywhere we wanted and do anything we wanted?" We were only beholden to two dogs and a cat. We knew that kids needed homes, and we were being called to open our homes, hearts, and lives up to teenagers, but it was *way* easier before all of this. But again, I don't believe easy is where the magic happens.

This is also not to say that kids aren't wonderful and great and that our lives aren't much more full, funny, and intense now, but dang if it wasn't easier without having to care for other humans. These kids are worth it. Every hard thing I've ever done has been worth it. There are hard things I can't believe I've done. Recently, I was talking with one of my best friends about when I sold all my stuff and moved to Brazil, and I was like, I would *never* do that now. I'd never have the guts. I just decided to go, and things fell into place, and it was all worth it. No one told me beforehand that I'd be the loneliest I've ever been, I'd be fearful for my life often, I'd have to battle softball sized tarantulas on the daily, I'd go eight straight months without a warm shower, or that the Wi-Fi would go out all too regularly, cutting off all my communication with everyone I knew and loved back in America. After reading that list, would you choose to move to Brazil? Doubt it. I wouldn't either! But what if I told you that you'd have more joy than you ever had, you'd form lasting, deep friendships, you'd learn to speak another language, you'd laugh easier than ever before playing Uno underneath a full moon, and you'd get to run through absolute downpours singing Justin Bieber at the top of your lungs with six Brazilian teenage girls, knowing that in that instant everything was exactly as it should be in the world?

Please don't think I'm living life on the edge constantly. I'm in bed by 9 p.m. every night, there's only so much a daredevil can do before 9 p.m. And maybe because of that, early bedtime confession, it is on my heart and mind to remind you of how amazing you are. You may say, "No I'm not!" And without even knowing you deeply, I'd argue otherwise. The millions of cells, muscles, tissues, bones, and organs that are put together to make you, you, and to open your eyes every morning and choose to do all the things that you do— be a stay-at-home parent, be a working parent, be a high-level executive, be a grocery store clerk, live with your parents, be a full-time student, be someone that loves plants—there are hard things in all of these choices.

Again, if you can feed the six metaphorical chickens you have, you can feed the thirty-six metaphorical chickens you have. In every aspect of life, there are hard things and you're doing them every day. Today, the fact that most of us are waking up every day and not choosing violence or anger is a dang miracle. The world is too crazy right now, people are getting hurt left and right, and you can't hardly sneeze without offending someone, and it is hard. I wrote this essay in year two of the pandemic, and I won't say anything because whatever it is, chances are it won't age well, but this right now, two years in, is hard! We are waking up, we are hopefully at least minimally tending to ourselves, our loved ones, our plants, our animals. Some days we aren't though. Some days it's too hard.

I feel you. Similar to my parents sitting me down and saying if I wanted to stay in my childhood bedroom for the rest of my life, they'd allow me to, I'm giving you permission to not ever do hard things again. If that's the permission slip you need, here it is signed on the dotted line. I have talked about writing this book for ten years. I told a friend a few months ago that part of the reason I didn't want to even begin writing this book is because what the heck comes after it. Do I stop dreaming big after that? I think everyone would give me that permission slip. There would be tangible and physical outcomes of my hard work and labor along with blood, sweat, and tears, and I think that would be enough. I have no idea what will happen after these big dreams get accomplished, or heck, how they even *will* get accomplished, but I have a sneaking suspicion that I will keep dreaming bigger dreams and figuring out how to accomplish them!

17

I'm Not Inspirational

I'm not inspirational. If I had a dollar for every time, I was told I was inspirational, I would be sending all my friends to space in our own rockets because I'd be so rich. The world loves to label people with disabilities and medical conditions as inspirational. Living my life with surgeries and medical devices doesn't make me inspirational. Simply existing as a person in a world and society that doesn't understand me and doesn't accept me isn't inspirational. I think we've twisted the meaning of inspirational. It has become something that drips of pity and sadness, and sometimes relief that our lives aren't as sad as others. Look at that person; they are so *inspirational,* but if you actually look at their lives . . . chances are, they aren't doing anything inspirational.

I'm not throwing shade at anyone, but oftentimes when that phrase is used, it's not because anything extraordinary is happening. My friend Ryann is in a wheelchair, and every day she is told she's inspirational as she wheels through the grocery store putting snacks in her basket. Sorry, y'all, that's not inspirational (she fully knows this, but for some reason, others don't). No one is inspirational as they simply go down the cheese aisle of Food Lion. On the other hand, she is a full-time nurse and is told she's inspirational as she wheels down the halls on a night shift. You know what the difference is? Being a nurse has always been her dream, and I think it's inspiring to be a nurse and so selflessly help others and to fight for your dreams regardless of what else is going on. I bet there have been other people in wheelchairs that have seen her, or articles written about her, who have been inspired because they've never seen anyone working in a hospital in a wheelchair, and maybe that's their dream too. Do you see the difference? One is filled with pity and a twinge of gratitude that your life isn't her life, and one is a fierce fight for your dreams–wheelchair or not. One evokes condolences, and one gets you moving and thinking about how to pursue your own dreams.

At this point, I can share almost anything on social media: movement related workouts, marriage stories, parenting/foster care/adoption posts, or just feel-good stories, and I'll be flooded with comments of *You're so inspiring*! Usually, if I get messages from strangers saying this, I'll ask what they saw in me or in a post that inspires them, and is it inspiring them to take action in their own lives?

Things I'm *okay* inspiring people to do:

- become foster parents
- move their bodies every day
- live the rebellious life they want to live
- chase, create, and choose joy daily
- have the hope that your hopes and dreams are worth pursuing
- love your body
- adopt more cats and chickens
- learn new skills at any age (I just learned how to use eyeshadow and curl my hair)

I like inspiring people. I like seeing lives changed because they saw my life and saw me unapologetically living the very best way I know how, and they decided they could too. I frequently get messages that people have started moving because they see me moving every day online, and that makes my heart soar. I know the very real benefits of daily, intentional movement. It's reduced my stress, reduced the urge to yell at everyone in my household, made me feel stronger, given me time to listen to inappropriate podcasts, time to feel the sun on my skin, etc.

Knowing that others are experiencing these things as a result of intentional movement is the most delightful thing

I can think of. I know it has a ripple effect. They start moving and feeling good, and then they tell their partner or parents or friends, and maybe they begin to move together. Then another life is changed. They are motivated by me and inspired by me, but I'm inspired by them because it is hard to do a new thing and to share about a new thing, especially when you can fail.

A year ago, I shared how I had an entire book proposal and sent it to at least thirty lit agents and then got rejected over and over and over. I don't regret sharing this because I worked really hard on it, and maybe others were inspired to do the hard thing they were putting off, and maybe they had more success.

The cycle continues and becomes like a snowball rolling down a hill. My intentional movement made me want to share with others, others picked up on it, they told others, and maybe someday, everyone, including my own family, will be moving their bodies every day. I think the world may be a happier place if that's the case. I just re-read this paragraph and it sounds really self-serving. It reminded me of the *Friends* episode where Phoebe and Joey are trying to find a truly selfless act, and Phoebe lets the bee sting her. I don't move to be inspiring. I started my movement journey before I even had social media. Instagram could blow up tomorrow, and I'd still be moving and talking about it to my real-life friends and family. If no one besides the people in my household knew I was moving my body every day, again, I wouldn't stop. Inspiring people to move is a by-product of my own movement journey, not the other way around. My life exists because I created it so intentionally to be a life of joy, big dreams, and a lot of love. My life does not exist to inspire people, but if they are so inspired to action along the way, cheers to them. I can't control how people respond and react to me; I can only control myself, so if people want to live their lives and tell me how inspirational I am, so be it. Hopefully, someday, that inspiration will spill out into action in their lives, and that'll be great! I have gone viral a few times over the past few years due to news outlets discovering me on social media and doing stories on me. The first time I went viral the stories started in the UK and ultimately culminated with Fox News picking up the story. As I had never been in the public eye like this before, I didn't know you shouldn't ever read the comments, especially on Fox News stories. Most of the comments were offensive, inaccurate, and rude but one comment legitimately made my heart stop for a minute for how much I loved it. "She is horrible at this whole 'being a victim' thing. I like her!" *Oh my gosh*! I have no idea who this person is, but I love them. Funny, sassy, and totally gets me. If you wrote that comment, let's be best friends. This comment is just so funny to me. I have never heard anyone describe my life this way, but it sums it up totally perfectly. Honestly, we all know people who are disabled or totally able-bodied who love to play the victim. Everyone's lives have circumstances that are beyond their control, and we can either figure out how to overcome them and press on, or we give in, blame others, blame the world and the systems we exist in, and give up and give in. I'd implore you to not choose the second option.

I can't force you to not be inspired by me, or by anyone else. I don't blame you for being inspired either. I see adaptive athletes on social media all the time kicking ass and have to catch myself before I leave them a comment saying that they've inspired me simply because they exist. I love inspiring people to action, and honestly, I think most others do too. The dopamine hit of someone saying, "oh my gosh look I bought a disco ball because you share every day when the sunlight hits yours and the joy it brings you seemed so fun, I wanted one too!" is unmatched. Go inspire people to action and tell them why they've inspired you to action–it makes the world may more fun!

18

I'm Tired

Disabled people are tired. We are tired of fighting. Recently the *Washington Post* published an article about the hashtag #DisabledLivesAreWorthy. Why are we still having to have articles in major publications about this? Why is it still being debated? This is why we are tired. We have to fight every dang day to have our voices heard, to get trending hashtags, to write articles so that able-bodied people can understand how we feel in a world that isn't built for us, doesn't want us, and would probably prefer to stop hearing about us. For some reason, despite being the world's biggest minority group, we are still a shock to people. We are still asked to be hidden away, to be institutionalized, to limit our exposure to society so that people don't feel uncomfortable. I'm not against able-bodied people. For the most part, besides how I look and the tubes that stick out of me, I pass as a very able-bodied person.

This topic is complicated and nuanced, and honestly, my feelings about it change daily. Does putting myself out there mean I have to answer the questions I get asked daily on social media and in real life? Nope. I don't owe anyone anything, even if I choose to brazenly put my tubes out in the world. I can exist and take up digital and physical space and not have to answer for anything. When did we come to the collective agreement that it was okay to ask people their personal medical history or to ask how people do certain things in life? Some days I'm a wealth of knowledge and feel generous and share all the things on social media and answer all the questions. Some days I don't. I know, it's frustrating and tricky. I know you earnestly want to know.

Well, you know what? I'm over it. I'm tired of hiding. I'm tired of worrying if other people are uncomfortable because of how I look. I'm tired of worrying every time I go in a store or airport or to a park if I'll be stared at or judged or mocked. I'll let you in on a secret though: Sometimes I still choose to hide myself. Not for the comfort of others, but because I hate it when Brandon or my kids have to explain why I look the way I do to others. If I'm in the mood and have the time, I don't mind doing it myself, after the literal ten millionth time in my life. But my kids have only been with me for, at the most, four years. They aren't used to all the stares, questions, confusion, or anger that can come from my existence. They are the best boys. They love me *so* fiercely. I hate when we are at karate or a football game and another kid will elbow my kid and ask, "Is that your mom; what's wrong with her?" and my kids have to explain or defend me. From the day they've moved in, we've been so open with them about asking me questions and talking about me with others. Sometimes they respond with silly responses, sometimes serious; sometimes they ignore questions just like I do. I let them lead the conversation and choose how they want to respond and explain. It's my story to tell, but when my kids are involved, they are the ones in charge. I hate the thought that my kids would ever be treated differently or made fun of because of me. That thought alone makes me want to hide. Part of me is like, *"Hannah they will be stronger and better humans if they learn how to stand up for themselves—and you."* But the part of me that typically wins out is, *"My kids have had really hard lives and have been through more shit than kids should ever go through, and if me hiding my face behind a book or coming in to pick them up at practice at the last minute instead of sitting on the bench watching them, lessens the number of questions they experience, then that's what I'll do."*

Okay, I know what you're going to say now. You're going to say, "But Hannah…I thought we were *supposed* to ask questions? How do we learn if we don't ask questions? If we aren't learning about disability from disabled people, how can we properly learn?!" Listen Linda, I don't know.

I will give you this though—sometimes questions are okay. Whaaaaat? I know. You are welcome to ask the questions. You are not welcome to be pissed when I don't want to answer them. I actually don't walk around and ask people at the grocery store checkout line when was the last time they had a pap smear or colonoscopy. I mean, do you? My diagnosis is my medical history, just like your pap smears are. If you wanna go around sharing that info, awesome. I'll be happy to learn. Actually, I won't—that's gross, let's not share that kinda stuff. But that's on you if you want to share! Just like it's on me if I want to share personal medical details with you. Chances are, if you're a kid, or have your kid genuinely ask me, "What's wrong with your face?", I'll tell ya! Kids are more fun to talk to anyway! And you know what I'll say? I was born this way! And kids are usually like, "Oh, okay cool." Then sometimes they say, "Why are your teeth so big?!" and I'll be like, "They are normal sized, but you can see a lot of them, can't you? Can you smile really big so I can see all your teeth too? Your teeth are so cool!" That's usually the end of the conversation. If your kid very enthusiastically asks, "What's wrong with her?" in line at Old Navy, don't shhh them. Tell them exactly what I just said, "People are born differently." You don't have to know someone's medical history to tell your kid that not everyone looks the same, sounds the same, talks the same, or moves the same. This is why representation matters. Read books about disabled kids (believe me, they exist!), watch movies with disabled characters, volunteer in places where people are unlike you. If you're reading this and have never talked to your kids about the fact that there are people who exist in the world that are different from them, do it.

Open up Instagram.

Search hashtags like #DisabledLivesAreWorthy.

You have access to a whole world that my generation didn't. I didn't grow up seeing other people like me. I didn't think this kind of representation existed, but you and all generations to come after us get to. Don't waste those resources. Once I posted a video stating what my condition is and still got asked what my condition is. This is why I'm exhausted. Disabled people are speaking; people probably just aren't listening.

Learn better, know better, do better. We are tired of being the guinea pigs. We are tired of being hidden away. I want my kids, their classmates, and their friends to not think twice about why their mama looks how I look. I want the world to be a kinder and more inclusive place for all of us to land.

19

Becoming a Supermodel

A few years ago, a local designer asked me to participate in Richmond, Virginia Fashion Week—I honestly thought she was crazy. I'm very far from what anyone would call *model material*. Emma insisted I walk in her show and quickly promised me I would not have to wear heels. She shared with me that her brand, *Evolve*, was living up to its name. The mission statement of *Evolve* is:

At <u>Evolve,</u> we believe in creating a space for people of all shapes, sizes, ages, races, gender identities, backgrounds, and abilities because to us, Beauty Has No Limits . . . It is our central mission to create a place where everyone feels like they can show up, exactly as *they are.*

Admittedly, I was skeptical. It is so easy these days to be trendy by claiming diversity, though many brands are falling flat. As Emma and I talked more and I watched her past shows and looked at her collection, I was sold. Little did I know this show would drastically change my life.

The day of the show had arrived. I went to a salon to get my hair and make-up done. I walked into a room full of women I've never met before and was met with kindness and smiles, but that was the least of the welcoming gestures. Not a single girl looked like anyone else. There were girls of all shapes, sizes, races, and abilities. There were a few other girls with medical conditions or disabilities. People often treat us differently, patronize us, and often treat us like infants or someone to be pitied. Not once did I feel that way or see anyone else treating anyone else in the room like that. Immediately, I knew the brand was the real deal. Honestly, I've never been in a room so diverse. I could tell how intentional and thoughtful Emma had been in selecting her models, and all my fears of not looking like a model were assuaged.

Getting made up is usually uncomfortable for me. I don't own a single hair product or a single piece of makeup. Due to medical issues, my lips don't touch, and I'm not able to close my eyes. Luckily, no lipstick was involved in this show. I'm a disability rights advocate by trade and spend my days advocating for others, but I often struggle to do so for myself. I have felt embarrassed and shameful of my body and what it can or cannot do and how it looks.

Even just being in that room of women empowered me to speak up for what I felt like I needed.

When I met my amazing makeup artist, from the start, I told her I couldn't shut my eyes, but I could hold them shut, or she could hold them shut, whatever she needed to do. She literally did not bat an eye or act annoyed or surprised at all. She was so kind and made the process of getting my makeup done so easy. She was a dream, and I'm so grateful we were put together. I was scared to look in the mirror when she was done for fear I'd hate what I saw. Since I don't wear makeup often, when I do, I tend to think I look like a clown. But that day, I was done up in a way that really did empower me and made me feel even more confident than I already am. She really knew what she was doing. Emma had the vision of keeping the girls looking natural and beautiful, and I'm so grateful. There was some time between having my makeup and hair done, so I had to call Brandon and show him how incredible I looked, and I walked around Target feeling like the biggest supermodel ever. Getting my hair done was so fun, and I left the salon feeling fierce, powerful, and ready to walk the runway.

We rehearsed walking down the runway and posing. The runway was this awesome brick walkway with fountains and a fake Eiffel Tower at the end. There were luscious plants and lights, and the audience sat in a horseshoe shape around the runway. The set was natural and beautiful and perfect for my first runway. I quickly found out most of the girls had modeled before, which would have intimidated me if I had known that beforehand.

But there was so much natural encouragement, I had no nervousness at all. I quickly learned how to pose for the various camera angles and was ready to go.

Showtime came, and I wore this incredible plaid coat and leather leggings. Right before I stepped onto the runway, I got really nervous, but there was no turning back. I threw my shoulders back and walked the runway with my head held high. There were people everywhere, cameras everywhere, and music bumping, but honestly, it all melted away as I was walking. I got to the end of the runway, did my three poses, and turned to walk back down. I'd never been to a fashion show before, so I had no idea the crowd would cheer for me, but they did. Their encouragement and cheers made me stand even taller as I took my final steps off the runway. The photographer at the end of the runway gave me a little thumbs up and mouthed, "Great job," as I walked off. Maybe he did that for all the girls, but I'd like to think he did it just for me as some extra encouragement.

The final part of the show involved all the models. We did a final walk down the runway, and we all had mirrors in our hands. When we were all in our positions, we flipped our mirrors over to face the audience. On our mirrors, we had previously written words of empowerment and encouragement such as, "I am strong," "I am fierce," and "I am wonderfully made," to remind the audience that not only were we all these adjectives, but everyone in the audience was too. Emma put so much thought and intentionality into celebrating and honoring everyone. Most fashion shows are all about the models and the clothes represented, but Emma really focused on empowering everyone that participates.

The show ended, and I put my boring normal clothes and Crocs back on and headed out to my beat-up minivan. The magic of the day was fading, but I was more pumped up than ever. I felt so excited and empowered and had that endorphin boost that only comes after you conquer something new. I was so proud of myself and so thrilled at how fun the day was, even though I had been so nervous going into it. All day, it felt like I kept checking off more and more boxes: showing up, entering rooms without knowing a single person in them, getting makeup and hair done, quickly learning how to walk a runway, spending a few hours making new friends and then being a model. These were all new and uncomfortable things for me, but I did them all, with no meltdowns. That in itself was a victory to me. I drove home pumping some jams and feeling so fulfilled. Trying new things and proving to yourself you can do things you previously thought you couldn't do is such an incredible feeling. Going into the day, I didn't know I would have such high emotions about the day, but it definitely far surpassed my expectations.

Later that evening, I saw an Instagram story of a video someone had taken of me walking down the runway, as well as some preliminary photos. I broke down in sobs. Not because I looked amazing (though I did) but because I have *never* seen a single person that looks like me walk down the runway. My whole youth was spent watching *America's Next Top Model* and *Project Runway* and reading *Teen Vogue,* and I promise you; I've never seen a supermodel with a tracheostomy tube or a feeding tube or facial abnormality. That night, I cried for all the girls and boys that will see my picture on the runway and realize they can do anything.

It was never my dream to be a model or to be on the runway, but it has to be someone's dream. Somewhere, some boy or girl who looks different may think they will never get to be a model or walk the runway because of how they look. They have gone their whole lives without seeing someone who looks like them, so they believe it's not possible for them either. Representation matters. I know there are people with disabilities and medical conditions that have modeled and walked the runway, and major brand campaigns are starting to be more inclusive, but for me personally, I had never seen anyone with as many tubes or abnormalities as myself.

My hope is, now that I've gone first and those videos and photos are all over social media, someone else will see them and know their dreams are possible. Inclusion matters. Representation matters. I am forever grateful for Emma reaching out to me and knowing the value of inclusion and representation and forming a fashion brand after those values. I still don't think I am model material, but if I have more opportunities to be on runways or in front of cameras, I will take those opportunities because I want every single person to know they belong in every space, including the fashion world.

20

Hold On to Your Elderberries

I'll admit, this essay seems to be a bit of an outlier. Here I am sharing funny animal stories, growing up stories, yelling at people who are ableist stories, and then ka-blam! A story all about business. I'm fairly certain I warned you that I was the biggest mystery the world has ever known, and that is just the truth. I never thought I'd be an entrepreneur or business owner. In fact, both times I've typed business in this paragraph, they have been spelled wrong (It's a hard word to spell, like restaurant—autocorrect fixed that one!).

I'm a dreamer, always down to make a buck or two, but I never thought those qualities would translate into a #bossbabe. I'm just kidding. I literally hate that phrase—don't ever call me that. Though, sometimes I do call

Brandon a boss babe because he's the one that does like 95 percent of our business stuff. I share this chapter because I believe seeing marginalized folks thriving is powerful. People like me can be successful entrepreneurs, and yes, they can enter any space and, indeed, belong there.

We own a business called Hannah's Handcrafted LLC. Very original I know. Maybe someday we will rebrand, but the alliteration is good, and, so far, it hasn't been a hindrance to our success, so it can stay for now. Here's our elevator pitch: *We make and sell high quality elderberry products ranging from elderberry syrups and jellies to household items such as candles, salt scrubs, tea, and an all-purpose chap balm for your body.*

By now you've probably realized that Brandon and I are not crafty, per se, but more homestead-y-ish. We love trying to make or grow our own food and products. We've had long stints of making kombucha (and teaching others too!), making kefir, making hot sauces, brewing beer, making wine in our bathroom, making jellies and preserves from our own fruit trees and bushes, making cheese out of our own goats' milk; you get the idea. Some of these have been successful and really fun; others have been somewhat disastrous but also really fun, like the time we forgot about the kombucha, and it fermented too much, and then we drank it and accidentally got drunk off it! See also: bathroom wine. We have never made any of these things for profit, purely for the enjoyment of trying new things and maybe having the outcome of an edible product.

Some hippie, crunchy friends introduced me to elderberries. On a whim, when I had a sore throat, I bought some at CVS. I took the recommended dosage and handed it to God. Within two hours, I felt totally better. I even have the original picture I posted on Instagram saved on my phone from that day. I was just like, *oh my gosh, friends, this really works*! I was hooked! Being the curious chaps that we are, Brandon and I thought, oh surely, we can make this ourselves! We started googling some recipes. We loved reading over different ingredients and their holistic properties and trying out different flavor combinations. We tried a few different recipes, and Brandon came up with his own concoction—we were obsessed.

I started using it daily and spreading the word to friends. I started making a batch a week to sell to pals that winter—when colds and flu season hit. We started preparing them for people to pick up mason jars from our front porch. They'd leave money under our doormat. When we started out, we weren't making much of a profit as it was pretty much made to order, but quickly, we started making bigger batches at a time, and our profits grew! Word started to spread about how good and how beneficial our product was. Every week we'd make more and more. I posted on a Facebook moms' group that I was selling it, and we were accidentally flooded with orders. It was, and is, so awesome to hear testimonials of our syrup helping sick kiddos or family members in a time of need. We were using real, whole ingredients, to make something that was actually making people feel better when they were ill. It was awesome. We still have the notebooks and sticky notes: Sarah: one 16 oz. jar, Heather: two 32 oz. jars, Sue: one 8 oz. jar." I'd feverously scribble these orders to Brandon when Facebook messages would pop up, and we'd promise to get them out the door shortly.

On December 18, 2019, I emailed our friend, who owned our favorite local coffee shop and sold tons of local products, asking if we could sell our elderberry syrup in her coffee shop. She was so generous and said, "I also thought about how this would be a perfect thing to sell at Perk. My only apprehension is that it's not from a licensed kitchen, and we are restricted from selling anything for consumption that has not been permitted by the state health department. I'm sorry, but if you ever do get a permit, I will be the first to stock it here at Perk!" That was all it took for us to figure out (with lots of help along the way) how to start a business and make elderberry syrup for real!

Brandon cashed out his 401(k) for all the business startup costs. I'm not saying that's the best thing in the world to do, as we got penalized on our taxes the following year, but we were all in. We believed so strongly that we could do this. We had made an overwhelming amount of money just selling off our front porch, and we knew this could work. February 19, 2020, we got licensed and certified as a real business that could make and sell products across state lines!

Along the way, we met amazing women who helped with our graphic design and labels and got us into markets. Please don't think we did this alone; we met incredible people along the way who helped make this newly found dream a reality. Now, nearly every week, we get new wholesale accounts, gain new customers because of word of mouth, and get tagged in posts asking for recommendations about which elderberry syrup to get.

Even if you're not a businessperson and don't care about any of this–listen to this: Be a person who mentions other people's names in rooms they aren't in. That is the biggest blessing anyone can have in life. We wouldn't be where we are in our business, in foster care, in running a nonprofit, in the careers we are in, without people mentioning our names to others. I'm not being annoying and talking solely about "networking." I'm just building real connections with people, and those conversations will happen, and people will remember you. Be a person who mentions other people and appreciates when it happens for you too. We need each other.

The day we "opened" our business, I literally googled how to ship glass jars. We had *no* idea what we were doing. We were using old Amazon boxes and newspapers and sending things out with a hope and a prayer. I downloaded a map of the United States and printed it out and taped it above our family desktop computer. I started coloring in the states we shipped to in a red colored pencil, and pretty quickly there was more red on the map than white. Friends and family from all over, and people that googled, us continued to buy our elderberry. We had *no* idea how to keep up with demand, how to predict how much to make in the commercial kitchen, and how to not spend eight to ten hours in said kitchen. We were constantly reworking our strategy and coming up with new ideas. Within six months of starting the business, our product line had expanded from two to four products and we partnered with another small business to source some ingredients.

We were doing five farmers' markets a week while working our full-time jobs and shipping orders every day. Looking back on it, I have no idea how we managed. Granted, we only had one kid at the time, so it was slightly easier, but dang. I do not do farmers' markets now because we have employees—EEK! Sometimes I forget how incredible it is that we started a business a month before COVID came to the United States, and two years later, we have employees! The empire is slowly growing. We've shipped to all fifty states and over ten countries. We are in stores across the east coast. Our products have been featured in magazines and won local awards. For two people who never thought they'd own a business to do this . . . we are really dang proud.

21

Which Box Do I Check?
Disabled or Medical Condition?

This is my least favorite essay to write. It's not fun. Maybe that's why it's at the end. I wanted you to see who I've become before you see the person I have been on this journey of life. I don't like the person I was when a lot of things in this essay happened and don't like the thoughts I had. But they are honest, and when we know better, we do better, so here I am doing better whilst sharing my very real experiences so you, maybe, can learn better too.

Throughout this book you've seen me refer to myself as disabled. This is a very recent development in my life. Up until age thirty, I never called myself disabled, never said I had a disability, and didn't identify with the disability community. When speaking about myself, I'd say, "Oh, I have a medical condition, or I was born with a medical condition" but never would say anything else. I know there is a hot debate between person first language and disability first language (i.e., person with autism vs autistic person), but that never really worked for me. Medical condition afflicted person is a mouthful to say. Do you want to know a secret? I was ashamed to use the term disabled and disability when referring to myself. None of what I'm sharing is how I feel now, nor am I particularly proud about my thoughts, but I'm nothing if not honest.

Growing up, my parents never used the words disability or disabled when referring to me. They'd say I had a medical condition or that I was born with a facial anomaly. I picture myself as a little girl trying to say anomaly like Nemo when he is trying to say anemone. There is not a time I can recall where my parents, nurses, doctors, or anyone used the term disabled in reference to me. I'm sure there were times when I was referred to as the r word, but I can't remember any. Besides going to mainstream kindergarten, I attended special education pre-school, not because of any physical or mental delays, but because I needed specialized nursing care. Even in that setting, I knew I was different. I didn't seem like other disabled kids. I was able to do anything and everything asked of me. I didn't need help walking or talking. The separation in my mind had already begun. They were disabled; I was simply born with a medical condition.

While the separation was real in my mind, it was never a lesser than or better than thing. I felt like I needed less help or support than others with disabilities did, but I wasn't better because of that. My parents certainly taught us that we all had value, we were all loved, and that everyone was important. We were raised to believe that God loved all of us and made us all equal. Yet, somewhere during childhood, and within the ableist society we live in, I learned to associate disabled with lesser.

I never fully believed that per se, but I was also mindful that nothing about the identifier of "disabled" felt applicable to me. As a kid, I was in gifted classes, involved in many extracurricular activities, and besides going to speech lessons, was totally "normal" (whatever that meant). When I was in elementary school, my mom taught at the same school we attended, so all the teachers already knew me because I was around the school before and after school every day with my mom. Before new school years would start, sometimes my mom would make little introduction packets or a little presentation about me and how I'd use an IV pole to hang my gravity food bag to eat through my feeding tube in the classroom and why I had a nurse with me in the classroom. When kids would ask me questions on the playground, I'd just tell them I was born different, and kids usually just care about having an answer to their question more so what the answer may actually entail.

When I was younger, my mom bought me a necklace; it was a little wooden girl wearing a green shirt and an orange baseball hat. She had brown hair and brown eyes like me, with Hannah written across her shirt. My mom told me to wear this necklace when I was meeting new friends in the neighborhood or at Girl Scouts or on the first day of school in case people couldn't understand what I was saying when I offered up my name. As I got older, she got me a gold necklace with Hannah shaped in gold wire, you know, because I was a classy broad.

Looking back, my parents went so above and beyond to make sure I was known, accepted, cared for, and loved, not just by my classmates but by the whole community. They worked so hard for me to access the right medical care, equal education, involvement, and accommodations in any activity I wanted to participate in. My childhood lacked nothing, though I did have an abundance of surgeries and medical appointments, but that was just normal for me. As an adult, especially a Disability Rights Advocate, now I'm like yes hello Hannah, having accommodations, having a nurse in the classroom, having parents and community members who advocated for me, these are all things that disabled people have. As a kid, I didn't know any different and again, no one ever used those words around me, so I had no idea this was extraordinary.

In undergrad, I majored in American Sign Language (ASL) and Deaf Studies, so I was surrounded by Deaf professors, classmates, and community members. American Sign Language was actually the first language my parents taught me, and it came to me naturally. I love ASL and expressing myself through sign language. College never really presented a struggle for me because it was abundantly clear that I was not Deaf, therefore not like the people I was frequently interacting with. The real internal conflict began for me in grad school. Like most budding social workers, I was becoming a social worker to help people! I knew I was interested in working with the disability community but had no idea what that would be like or how I'd personally be impacted by this decision. Again, I still was not considering myself a member of the disabled community. Oh, how naive I was.

My first internship in grad school was at a brain injury clubhouse. Adults with brain injuries were able to come during the day and volunteer, learn living skills, work on job skills, and socialize with other adults with brain injuries. As an intern, I worked with the administrative staff working on fundraising, event planning, grant research, and other macro social work tasks. At one point, I was out in the community collecting gift cards and other donated items for an upcoming silent auction fundraiser.

One particular business was a rehabilitation facility that helped people with physical or occupational therapy, brain injury rehab, stroke rehabilitation and other important services. I explained that I was an intern with the brain injury clubhouse, and I was there to pick up their donated items. The woman behind the desk couldn't understand me well and thought that I was a brain injury survivor needing services. I spoke very slowly and clearly about who I was and what I was there for, and she just kept telling me I had to register for services. There was no convincing her otherwise that I was there for other purposes than obtaining services. I speak to strangers every day, but sometimes it just doesn't click, and if someone has an idea in their head of what I'm trying to say, it's hard to convince them otherwise. I texted my supervisor and asked if she could call the front office where I was to explain who I was and what I needed. There is nothing I hate more than inconveniencing anyone, and I felt so inadequate as an intern that I couldn't pick up a simple donation without needing assistance from my boss.

I couldn't believe this woman thought I was someone with a brain injury. She saw my car keys, she saw I wasn't accompanied, she saw I was using a cell phone–what the heck? How could I be someone with a brain injury? Excuse me, my ableism was showing. Brain injuries don't have a look. Brain injuries don't mean universally you can't do XYZ simply because you have a brain injury. There isn't, and wasn't, anything wrong with the people I was interning with, but I was trying to establish myself as a professional and distance myself from the clients I was working with to show those boundaries.

If I thought this would be the only time this would happen, I was definitely wrong. Every year in January, Virginia enters their legislative session. There was an advocacy day for brain injury services (which are severely lacking in Virginia). We took many of our clubhouse members with us and went over bills that we were going to ask senators and delegates to support and encourage members to share their personal brain injury stories. I was nervous to go to the General Assembly and speak with delegates and senators, but luckily, I was just ensuring we were where we were supposed to be and let the members shine in their advocacy skills by sharing their stories.

We went to several delegate offices and the clubhouse members were really making an impact, sharing their stories and impressing upon the delegates how important approving more services and finances for brain injury services in Virginia were. We went to our last appointment of the day, and all the members had shared their stories and pleas for the delegate to vote yes on bills that would provide much more funding for brain injury services. The delegate was very responsive and attentive to what the members had to say and was shocked to hear about the lack of important services they needed to live their lives in the community.

At the end of the meeting, the delegate turned to me and said, "We haven't heard your story yet, would you like to share how you got your brain injury?" and man . . . I didn't know I could blush, but I swear my face must have turned bright red. It felt like I was on fire. I had to immediately figure out how to say that I was an intern, without a brain injury, without making the clubhouse members feel like there was anything to be ashamed about having a brain injury. Fumbling over my words, I muttered something like, "Oh, no, I don't have a brain injury. I mean, I have a medical condition, but not a brain injury, and I'm an intern helping direct these meetings today, but there's nothing wrong with having a brain injury! I just don't have one!"

I don't really ever get embarrassed, but dang if I wasn't on this day. Luckily, the clubhouse members echoed me in saying I was an intern, and part of me hopes that the delegate realized how ableist and out of line he was acting in assuming that I too had a brain injury, but his face showed no recognition of doing or saying anything wrong. Welcome to ableism. He was also a politician and probably had a pretty good poker face, so I do hope that he realized the error of his ways and was more embarrassed than I was, but I doubt it.

I searched the faces of the clubhouse members to see if they were concerned about the interaction that just occurred, but they, too, were impassive. Rarely have I experienced such assumptions. I know we all assume, and I am hardly thinking that I don't fall into assumptions about people, but I don't tend to say them out loud in a room of people. The saying is true though; he for sure did make an ass out of himself and me. People do tend to assume incompetence when they see me, as if having a facial difference equates to any sort of developmental or intellectual disabilities. This is why representation matters. If we were more exposed to people of all abilities, we wouldn't have to make assumptions about them, their disabilities, medical conditions, or competency. Not that any of this is any of our business anyway. In that moment in the Capitol, if I had lived experiences with a brain injury, I surely could have shared my story and maybe our collective stories, and lobbying would have persuaded this delegate to vote in favor of more funding, but that's a pretty unique situation. On any given day though, people's lives and experiences have no bearing or impact on our lives, and assuming things about them does nothing but make us look like fools and waste our time and brain space.

In early adulthood I was still very far removed from the word disability. When I started my Instagram account and started virtually meeting disabled people, it honestly began to feel like a sliding scale. That person was very disabled, while that other person was a little disabled, and I still felt like I was outside the spectrum. My best friend, Ashley, has Cerebral Palsy and has always referred to herself as disabled, and I honestly used to try to fight her on it. I'd be like Ash, you're not disabled; you're amazing, brilliant, kind, funny, and the most capable and confident person. Again–welcome to my dumb ableism. As if disabled people can't be those things. I have thought really deep and hard about what I pictured a disabled person to be like, if I thought they weren't all these other things that I was seeing. I don't know. It's gross to think about and gross to admit to you, but I gotta be honest.

Once in conversation, Ash referred to me as disabled, and I got angry with her. The only time I ever considered myself as disabled was when I was filling out job applications. The internal debate would begin. If I check yes, I'm disabled, will that help my chances of getting hired because they have some diversity and inclusion quota to meet, or if I check yes, will it hurt my chances because they think disability = incompetent. Under the list of disabilities that the disabled checkbox encapsulated, other medical conditions were always listed, so I figured that did actually apply to me, so I'd check yes. I have no idea if it ever helped me or hurt me to get a job or not, but I would check it. I felt guilty. Like I was only using the term disabled for my own benefit but rejecting it in real life.

Eventually Ashley had some come to Jesus conversations with me about the word. She pointblank asked me what I was scared of if I referred to myself as disabled and why I was so averse to it. It took several days to get back to her because I had some real soul searching to do. It was so uncomfortable to have these thoughts and these conversations with Ashley and Brandon, but it was necessary. Clearly, I had been avoiding the issue the majority of my life, though I knew I needed to be gentle with myself in the process. I really hadn't grown up with these words and thoughts about myself, so it took a lot of courage and deep diving to think about this.

At work, I was serving people with disabilities every day, on social media I was learning, growing, and experiencing life with incredibly badass disabled individuals, and finally coming to the terms that I, too, was disabled was a bit of a jolt.

Me. Disabled.

My heart still feels like it skips a beat when I say that. It felt like learning a new language when I finally started using these words. Disabled was much easier to say than explaining that I had a medical condition, so that was nice getting to save words and explanations. The experience was similar to breaking in a new pair of jeans. Disabled fit me, but was a little tight, and needed a lot of breaking in. I had to practice saying I was a disabled woman. I had to ensure that I was saying it for the real and right reasons and not as means of getting anything from the world. Believe me, society affords a great deal of pity and sympathy to disabled people, and I was not trying to gain that, so it quickly felt natural.

In addition to not growing up with this term, and perhaps recognizing the stigma around it, part of my hesitancy to refer to myself as disabled was because of my marriage. Brandon loves me and accepts me exactly as I am, but it was easier to think that he was married to someone who happened to be born with a medical condition than the fact that he may be married to a disabled woman. I don't think he cares either way. He has afforded me the grace and ability to dissect this topic in my heart, soul, and mind, and he has adopted the language that I have chosen to adopt. Especially as we have these dreams of making the world more inclusive through an accessible playground and community garden in our town, he will talk about our project in terms of his disabled wife never seeing anyone like herself as a child and how we don't want that for other kids. I just want everyone's lives to be easier and not to be a burden or make anything harder for anyone, and knowing how ableist the world is, I don't want to inflict any of that nonsense on anyone else.

I reckon Brandon is perfectly capable of handling that though; in fact I know he is, based on his reactions to trolls on social media, so I'm not worried, but those feelings were really real, and they were and are valid. It's all a process. Some days I still say I have a medical condition, and some days I simply say disabled. Unlike a job application, normal conversation is fluid. I don't have to check one box in this life and never get to check another.

I think this applies to everything in life. We make commitments like marriage, but other than that, we get to choose every day who and what we want to be. I will always be disabled; that won't change, but if someday the term disabled no longer serves me, that's cool too. For right now, it feels comfortable and right to me as I exist and move through our society. Never in my wildest dreams did I think I'd be disabled (ha-ha, I always was) or that I'd refer to myself that way, but life has a funny way of surprising us, doesn't it?

Language used to refer to ourselves is extremely personal and intimate. This ranges the gamut from personal pronouns, gender, sexuality, medical diagnoses, disabilities, and other societal assumptions. Our society has gotten better in this department in some ways but has eons to go. My personal journey to accept and use the term disabled when speaking about myself took a long time and was very hard and confusing and intimate, and I'll be damned if anyone tries to assign anything else to me.

We need to be better listeners when people are speaking. Often it is abundantly clear how people would like to be identified if only we'd shove our own assumptions and biases aside to listen. Every single disabled person is about to stand up and shout amen at this next sentence.

Disabled isn't a bad word.

For a long time, I too thought it was, which sucks, but it's not. It's freeing. There is an entire community of disabled people all around you, as one in five people is disabled, and feeling that comradery is incredible. I went 28 years without ever seeing someone that looked like me, and then I met my friend Courtney on Instagram; she has my same condition, and when I was mindlessly scrolling and her posts come up, I had to do a double take because I thought it was me.

The feeling of seeing someone that looked like me for the first time ever brought me to tears. I don't believe in having regrets, but if I ever did, it would be that I regret that I went 30 years rejecting the title of disabled. The freedom I feel now could have been felt my entire life. I could have felt understood and sought out people who understood what it was like to be stared at everywhere they went, to have to fight to be understood and heard and accepted. Currently, I have a great group of pals with feeding tubes, whom I can text at any moment and say; hey, is this normal, or hey, have you experienced this, or hey, what works best for _____? THAT IS THE BEST!

Of course, I have lots of friends that I can text about ten million topics other than feeding tubes and disability related things, but to have that tribe who understands how annoying it is to ruin clothes daily with stomach acid that leaks out of you is next level.

Find your tribe, whatever that tribe looks like. We weren't made to do life alone, and chances are there are people on this planet of seven billion people who can understand what you're going through. It is worth it to fight for that community. For me, it was worth going through really hard and uncomfortable conversations and deep diving into myself to come to terms with saying I'm disabled. The more proudly I talk about it, the less stigma or shame can be associated with it. Ashley, I'm really glad you pushed me to think about this further. It's changed my life to come into an identity that I always had but never wanted to accept.

22
The Final Disco Hour

Here we are. The end of our time together. My only goal in writing this book was to extend hope to people that they can live the rebellious life they want. I hope I succeeded. If I encouraged you at all to pursue dreams, do hard things, adopt more cats, or at least gave you a laugh, then my job here is done. My life has been anything but ordinary, and I'm so grateful for it. As I've mentioned, I've had the idea to write this book for over ten years. Honestly. What the frick did twenty-one-year-old Hannah think she had to write about? No idea. At 32, I still don't really know, but I'm having a really fun time living and rebelling and creating joy along the way when I'm too tired to find it.

I truly do think the best is yet to come. My life isn't perfect. I hope I've painted an accurate picture of the highs and lows and everything in between here. You can do it all…if you want. Having wild dreams, living a comfortable life, adopting all the kids, living in a van. My bad hours are no worse than yours. We need to spend far less time comparing ourselves to each other. Spend time working on yourself, loving your people, cultivating hobbies, and drinking water.

We get this one life. I do not think anyone gets to the end of their life and says, "Wow, I am so glad I spent all that time wishing I was thin like that person, had a house like that person, was wealthy like that person, or pursued my dreams like that person." Life is too dang short, y'all. Use your one rebellious life to have the most fun. Do the things that make you happiest. When my friends share their problems with me or ask me advice, I have learned to say, "If you are happy, healthy, and whole in whatever situation you're in, then I'm supportive." That's how I feel about you! If you're happy, healthy, and whole or working towards that, then heck to the yeah. If you're not those things, I understand too. By most standards, I'm rarely doing most of those things (thanks feeding tube) but working every day towards them! I hope this book has inspired you to action, whatever that action looks like for you. You got this. I'm really proud of myself, and I'm really proud of you. Now go buy a disco ball or move your body.

Acknowledgements

Firstly, I would like to thank me, myself, and I because no one else wrote this book but me!

But then, I'd like to thank Brandon for inspiring a breakdown while on vacation and pushing me to do the dang thing and write this book. Thank you to my boys who make me laugh daily and held me accountable to writing every day (and distracted me!). This book would not have happened if Andrea Jasmin hadn't slid into my DMs one day, believed in this book, and waited a year and a half for me to write it. I still don't know how to use a comma, and she saved me. I'm so grateful for Shana Hartman and her incredible team for graciously agreeing to format this book and get it into your hands. Thank you so much to Katrina Taggart Hecksher for making my wild photoshoot dreams come true and letting me bring Chicken Lizzo into her brand-new photography studio.

Lastly, thank you to all of you over the years who have encouraged me to write a book, told me you'd read anything I wrote, and asked me every day if I had been writing. Without the encouragement, this book would only exist in my dreams.

Made in United States
North Haven, CT
25 January 2023

31652328R00114